Bes'

"A must-read for

has staf

G000038235

New

Manager

Secrets

How to accelerate your success as a
manager immediately

Alison Miles-Jenkins FCIPD

CEO and Founder of Leading Light Learning

London

New Manager Secrets

How to accelerate your success as a manager *immediately*

The 'must-have' real world guide for managers

Copyright ©2016 Alison Miles-Jenkins BA (Hons) FCIPD

First Published 2016   Alison Miles-Jenkins

Published in London, United Kingdom by Leading Light Publishing

The right of Alison Miles-Jenkins to be identified as the author of this book has been asserted in accordance with the Copyright, Designs and Patents Act 1988

All rights reserved. No part of this publication may be reproduced, stored in a retrieval system or transmitted in any form or by any means, electronic, mechanical, photocopying, recording, scanning or otherwise, except under the terms of the Copyright, Designs and Patents Act 1988, or without the written permission of the Publisher. Requests to the Publisher should be emailed to enquiries@leadinglightlearning.com in the first instance.

The publication is designed to provide accurate and authoritative information in regard to the subject matter covered. While all attempts have been made to verify the information provided in this publication, neither the author nor the publisher assumes any responsibility for errors, omissions, or contrary interpretations of the subject matter herein. The views expressed are those of the author alone. The reader is responsible for his or her own actions. Neither the author nor the publisher assumes any responsibility or liability whatsoever on the behalf of the purchaser or reader of these materials.

Copyright ©2016 Alison Miles-Jenkins
All rights reserved.
ISBN: 978-0-9935774-0-6
ISBN-13: 0993577407

DEDICATION

To the 1000s of managers who have attended my training courses, workshops and coaching sessions and have shared their challenges, frustrations and aspirations. Their subsequent success stories have inspired me to write this book and reach 1000s more who want to successfully get on or climb the management ladder.

To Lauren, Alex and Frankie who coped so well with having a career mum for all these years – I am so proud of you.

To my husband Gordon, who has been my rock, my friend and most ardent supporter. Without your love and belief in me much of this would not have been possible.

And finally, I dedicate this book to people all over the world who recognise that personal development is invaluable and always possible. It enables us to enrich our lives and those of others we interact with, at work, at home, at play. Ultimately it contributes towards a better world. What could be better than that?

Additional New Manager Secrets Resources

www.newmanagersecrets.com/resources to register for additional material mentioned in this book and other guidance

www.leadinglightlearning.com for our management development and training programmes, accelerator days and online membership

For one to one coaching with me please email: alison@leadinglightlearning.com

People say the nicest things.........

"A must-read for anyone who has staff."
Russell Brunson
Entrepreneur, Speaker, and winner of USA TODAY's Best-Selling
Author award

"This is the book for managers at any stage in their career who want
to get their hands on practical tips, techniques, skills and knowledge.
It answers all the 'how do I....' questions that managers face daily and
also gives the reader the chance to add their own reflections and
actions, distinctive of Alison's style. Alison has shared her huge
amount of expertise and experience, gained from many years
developing managers and leaders and poured it all into this book.
Highly recommended."
Liz Chasteauneuf
Learning and Development Manager, FM Conway Ltd

"This is a must read for managers! In my experience it is rare to have
a management book which provides such a relevant and practical
range of strategies, tips and skills for being a successful manager. I
recommend this book to those new to management and to those who
want to improve their management skills. Alison has dedicated her
career to helping managers and has poured her 25 years of
experience into what is a great handbook. If you manage people keep
a copy with you."
Chris Francis
Head of Property Services, Golding Homes

'Practical, powerful, readable'
"This is a book you can read all the way through, or you can dip into
when you need specific advice, for example on how to handle a
difficult conflict situation in your team. Alison has distilled her
academic and incredible working knowledge and expertise into this

highly practical and readable book. I loved the action plans that help you to really focus on implementation.

So it is the book I will recommend to my many clients who are working hard to develop their managers and deliver great performance - I'll also be using it regularly in my own business, to develop my own management skills and those of my team."

Jo Ayoubi

CEO, Track 360G5 - Fully customised 360 Degree Feedback

"I wish that this book had been available when I was a new manager. It is not full of complicated theories or long winded accounts of research, but it offers down to earth suggestions for the way forward for many common issues. It is an easy read and is also very useful as a reference book. Even after many years managing staff I found it helpful today to dip into when I was considering how to deal with a problem."

Karen Elley

Postgraduate Dental Dean, NHS Health Education West Midlands

"New Manager Secrets" will transform your management skills. With its focus on practical application of Alison's top techniques, tips and know-how, you can rapidly become a very successful manager – the sort that people want to work for and give their best to. It's a 'must have' for new or aspiring managers and a great aide-memoire for those experienced managers and leaders."

Carolyn Grinsted

HR Manager, Syngenta Bioline

CONTENTS

Preface   ix

Introduction: A note to you, the reader   1

Management Challenge Number 1:   5
Your first line management role and how to cope with the
first 100 days

Management Challenge Number 2:   23
How to recruit and select the best person for the job

Management Challenge Number 3:   43
How to start building a team

Management Challenge Number 4:   49
How to be the leader

Management Challenge Number 5:   55
How to get people motivated to do what you want them to
do

Management Challenge Number 6:   69
How to delegate for maximum return

Management Challenge Number 7:   77
How to run great team meetings

Management Challenge Number 8:   85
How to project personal presence and succeed at
presentations

Management Challenge Number 9:   95
How to communicate to get people on side

Management Challenge Number 10:   105
How to manage your time

Management Challenge Number 11:   117
How to performance manage

Management Challenge Number 12:   131
How to handle underperformance

Management Challenge Number 13:   145
How to handle difficult people and conflict

Management Challenge Number 14:   155
How to develop your team

Management Challenge Number 15:   175
How to manage Individual Contributors

Management Challenge Number 16:   179
How to get your team customer/client focussed

Management Challenge Number 17:   187
How to handle complaints

Management Challenge Number 18:   195
How to develop a winning mind-set

Management Challenge Number 19:   203
How to start climbing the management ladder

Management Challenge Number 20:   211
How to get to the room at the top

Conclusion: How To Guarantee Your Success   215

PREFACE

The very first line that popped into my head when starting to write this preface was from the Robert Palmer song, Oh, Mercy, Mercy Me: "oh, things ain't what they used to be, no, no". Perhaps not the first point you were expecting to read at the beginning of a management book, but then, this is not a typical management read. For two very important reasons. Let's explain.

What I know from 30 years immersing myself in learning about management and leadership, and dedicating my entire career to helping people like you become managers is that times have changed dramatically. Things literally 'ain't what they used to be.' Management theory and academic approaches aren't what many people need to start or progress their management career anymore. Fine in the University lecture theatre, but that's a million miles away from the current everyday work reality for most.

Here's the thing:

1) People no longer want or need lengthy programmes that take them away from work to focus on the theories, the academic models and the fluff.

2) Time is their most precious resource and implementation is key. So what they do want and need is to focus on the answers to the 'how to...' questions: the tips, techniques, shortcuts and tricks that are easy to implement and drive results.

So this book is very different. Firstly, it's all about the simple, practical stuff that makes that difference as a manager. It's what people see you doing, how you are doing it, the results you achieve and how you feel about yourself that can accelerate your success as a manager or a wannabee manager, and therefore your career and ultimately your life. So I've poured all my 'how to' experience and knowledge that I've worked really hard to achieve over almost 30 years into 'New Manager Secrets – How to accelerate your success as a manager immediately' so that you can read it in a day and start living it immediately.

Secondly, here's an awesome life changer – it still resonates as powerfully with me as on the first day I discovered it, and it's a key driver behind this book and the success you can achieve with it too:

To know and not to do is actually not to know

You might want to read that again a couple of times to yourself. It's become my most important mantra. We all know lots of stuff don't we, but if we don't actually apply it, we might as well not know it in the first place.

Implementation is key. That, together with the secrets, tips, techniques and magic touches I'm sharing in this book will, I guarantee, accelerate your success as a manager.

What's more, I've written this book in a way that, if you are serious about your potential success, you really can read it in a day. I did this because I know only too well that most people who purchase books today unfortunately never finish them. I really want you to finish this book, ideally in a day. Remember, there's over two decades of learning at the very least in this book, and you can acquire it in a single day. That's amazing isn't it? This is exactly the sort of book I so wanted and needed when I started out in my career but could not find.

What's more, you can start applying the techniques and making them work for you immediately. You may need to tweak here and there – after all practice makes perfect, but success, as I say, lies in action. Follow this book. Apply immediately, using my 4 'R's© approach: review, reflect, revise and reapply if necessary. Oh... and keep doing – consistently and persistently. You'll get results immediately. You'll build momentum. Before you know it, you'll get to where you want to go.

To your success as a Manager

Alison x

INTRODUCTION
A NOTE TO YOU, THE READER

No matter where you are in your career right now – whether you are a senior manager or you've just put your foot on the management ladder, or perhaps you are struggling to get noticed at work – here's what we all have in common: we want to improve our lives and the best way to do this is to improve ourselves. That's one of the reasons why the personal development industry is huge, on a worldwide scale.

Yet despite this, most people get up each day and life stays pretty much the same. I'm guessing you are not one of those people, or you wouldn't have bought this book. Now, if you haven't read the preface already, please go back and do so. I mention this because, if you are like me, you'll have skipped that bit in your enthusiasm to get going with the introduction to this book and all the secrets I'm going to be revealing. The thing is though I've shared some really powerful stuff in the preface that sets the scene for everything else and I don't want to bore those readers who read it first by repeating it now! So, go on, please just flick back a few pages and check out my preface before re-joining me here.

So now I'm assuming you've read the preface and you'll have got a feel for why this book is so different to the many other management books out there or maybe those gathering dust on your bookshelf.

1) **New Manager Secrets** reveals exactly what it takes to accelerate your success as a manager. Without the fluff, without the unnecessary theory. It's based on the very same practical techniques and skills I've shared with more than 45,000 people to help them be more successful at work. You can read this book in a day and discover everything you need to know to accelerate your management success that others have taken at least 10 or 20 years to acquire. So invest a day and save two decades. Think about how much time invested in learning this book will save you!

2) It's practical. I've poured 30 years' experience into powerful chapters of 'know-how' that have transformed how managers manage and that can change your life too.

3) I'll be encouraging you every step of the way to implement. So you can start applying the tips, techniques, short cuts and tricks immediately and see the results for yourself.

Here's an idea that works for me because, as an award winning people development expert, trainer, success coach, speaker and author I have to read a lot of books whilst also leading a very busy life too. Why not overcome one of the key reasons why people don't finish books and pick a target day and time to read it from beginning to end? You'll find I've made it as easy for you as I can.

New Manager Secrets is so much more than just a book, as I've included exercises, cheat sheets and key takeaways with every chapter. There are more than 220 key takeaways in total. These are practical actions you can start taking and seeing the results from immediately. I don't want you to keep this book in pristine condition. It's a tool so please use it. Scribble on it, fill in the questions and the exercises. Highlight sentences, fold the page corners over, whatever. I don't care. All I want you to do is to use it, implement it and start seeing the results. To maximise the impact I've also included for you some additional links to online resources and special supplementary videos for each of the really crucial bits too.

You'll discover stories about problems that others have faced that I'm sure you'll be able to relate to. The stories are real, they come from real people in real client organisations I've worked with. I've just changed the names and edited for clarity and confidentiality.

Achieving is very important to me. I built it into the name of my consultancy business that I started 25 years ago and it is still my key driver today. It's taken me a total of 30 years to discover what I am going to be sharing with you in this book. You can get it in a day. So if you are or want to be an achiever too, **New Manager Secrets** can be an absolute game-changer for you.

See you in Management Challenge 1: Your first line management role and how to cope with your first 100 days. It's relevant whether you are new to management or have some experience under your belt.

MANAGEMENT CHALLENGE NUMBER 1: YOUR FIRST LINE MANAGEMENT ROLE AND HOW TO COPE WITH THE FIRST 100 DAYS

The secrets it's best to know now

People often say that the beginning is a very good place to start. So Management Challenge No 1 sets the scene for those who are new to management; perhaps you've just got your first management role or you're looking to get started in management. Perhaps you work in a corporate organisation, the public sector, a charity or a start-up. Or maybe you run a professional practice – a lawyer, dentist, doctor, accountant for example and because you are successful you've expanded and you now have a team. Either way, this is for you. If you've been a manager for a while, perhaps now at a senior position, you could always skip this one. On balance though, if I were you, I'd still go through it. There's nothing like a fresh perspective now and again or some timely reminders to accelerate our success with something. If you have more junior or new managers reporting to you, then this section may help you put yourself in their shoes for a moment. It's always useful to do that now and again, isn't it? That way we protect ourselves from an 'unconscious use of skill' (because we think we are old hands at something) and instead place ourselves in the much more productive state of 'conscious use of skill' where we are more open to reflection, fresh ideas, improvement and renewed success.

The consistent management challenge

In fact, while writing this book, I have drawn on the range and depth of my own personal experience in management as well as the 25 years or so when I have been training and coaching others to be successful managers too. My first management role was 34 years ago now, at my very first job after graduating from Uni. On day 1 in the job I was unexpectedly made the supervisor of a trainee – a role which as you can imagine I knew absolutely nothing about - and I've not stopped developing my management and leadership skills since then. After all, leadership is a journey not a destination. Several roles later, I left a job heading up a training and development team and set up my own people management and development consultancy. So it's something I've been living and breathing ever since. So much has changed at work over that period. The core focus of being a manager has not. The challenge of "how do I get this group of individuals to perform effectively, willingly and consistently?" remains at the top of the agenda today. Technology and the workplace may at times have changed beyond recognition, but the same needs for engagement, motivation, and results have not. In fact as I write these very lines, productivity, cost control and managing performance are key concerns, according to the CMI[1] .

Your new management role

As with many things in life, the first step is often the hardest which is why I wanted to offer some help initially to those who are starting off on their first management role. If you are a first time

---

[1] Chartered Management Institute Infographic 2016

manager I'm sure you will often be faced with a variety of emotions and feelings ranging from excitement and eagerness to anxiety and apprehension. We all feel the butterflies in the stomach on the big occasions in life don't we and my aim with this section is to help the new manager to get those butterflies flying in formation, heading in the right direction and at the right speed! I remember in my first role the excitement of getting this unexpected and new management position was accompanied by feeling a big dose of uncertainty, nerves and self-doubt.

If you are new to the organisation, as I was all those years ago, you may also be faced with trying to establish what the culture and style of the place is like. The culture, values and style of an organisation are important things to consider as a manager. These things will provide opportunities and constraints as you are finding your management feet. You will also want to get to grips with the objectives and expectations of your new organisation. Whether you are new to the organisation or not, the first time manager needs to understand expectations. So here's some encouragement that made a big difference to me. There is some good news for the new manager: those who appointed you believe you are the right person for the job. You convinced them of this during the recruitment process after all, didn't you! They have confidence that you can do the job otherwise they wouldn't have given you this opportunity. It's their neck on the line if you fail. So remember this: your own line manager will want you to succeed otherwise you wouldn't be in the job. It's important to remember this, because at times it may not seem like it.

Some tips on getting started

So where do you start? A good place to begin is to review the information you have gathered throughout your recruitment process, whether you have changed employers or it's an internal opportunity. The research you did to find out about the organisational objectives and priorities will be very helpful in giving you a steer for what's expected of you now. Even the job advert can be a list of tasks, objectives and challenges that you, as the new manager, need to tackle. So take a look at the information you compiled during that recruitment process that got you the role and look too at the organisation's website. Somewhere there, hopefully easy to find, will be statements about what the organisation is there to achieve and why it exists. From my experience this isn't always readily shared with new managers – silly as that might sound.

What are the objectives for a new manager?

Having understood the wider organisational strategy and context, the next step is to work out how that applies to your role. Whatever level you are appointed to, you must make sure you have a clear understanding of the objectives for the role. We all have a boss, sometimes more than one. We are all accountable to someone so the first time manager needs to quickly get to grips with what their expectations are. A good boss will be clear about that, but it is not always straightforward. An early discussion with your boss about priorities and expectations will get this out in the open. You should have your own ideas gained from the recruitment process and now is the time to have that discussion to check understanding and be clear from the outset. It's really important because going forwards you'll be judged against expectations. I've found that in many organisations these are poorly communicated so it's hardly surprising things go wrong and disappointment and tension occur. Remember of course that you are going to have to communicate expectations to your staff too!

Some organisations have a cascade of objectives in the form of a Balanced Business Scorecard. This identifies the organisational objectives and cascades these objectives throughout the organisation. The concept here is that ultimately your objectives add to those of your department, which with the objectives of other departments will add up to the achievement of the corporate goals. All perfectly logical. In reality this wonderful logic may be not quite what it seems. The setting of objectives is a complicated business in its own right. Often what people see as a desired outcome is obscured by a poorly framed objective. You may at the very least have core competencies, organisational behaviours, specific role competencies and Key Performance Indicators (KPIs) to get to grips with too. If you are in a small business or start up these may not be in place.

Here's an example

Take for example a Contact Centre I worked with who had a target to answer all calls in 15 seconds. Fantastic customer service was the driver behind this. However, without a measurement of quality, the target could be achieved by simply answering the call and rushing the caller off the phone so that the call handler can get to the next caller. So this one dimensional approach resulted in a rather skewed and disappointing result. It had the best of intentions behind it but it was poorly framed. It led senior management to focus on why service performance was deemed to be so poor. The contact centre manager was under pressure to achieve the objective set but criticised for not thinking more widely and considering the customer experience. So get clear about your objectives but think about and ask about why these objectives are there too. What are they trying to achieve?

Here's a useful note to self: asking why is one of your key tools. Be careful here though because you can have too much of a good thing! If you ask "why?" repeatedly you can come over as aggressive, so ask why in different ways. Taking my contact centre example, you might explore this as follows: can you explain why the focus is on speed of answering? What about call handling quality? Are our customers asking for speed as the first priority or is there more to it?

Managing people for the first time

The good news is that one group of people who will also want you to succeed is your team. This might not at first appear obvious, but few people want to work in a team that is not performing well. So your people are likely to want to be part of a successful team and so will want you as the team leader to succeed. Of course, human nature being what it is, there might be some who don't want to be there but on balance people prefer success to failure. It can appear daunting to be managing people for the first time. Even if you initially have just one person you are responsible for it can be scary. So why not start by considering your team as a social group? When meeting people for the first time socially we often look for areas of mutual interest. One other aspect is that we instinctively assess people based on whether we see them as a threat to our interests or not.

A mistake to avoid from the word go

This instinctive social behaviour should not be forgotten just because we are starting off in management. Using this knowledge leads us to consider how we come across. It is a mistake to put on the cloak of management and then to think we have to come across as immediately decisive and full of initiative. These are laudable attributes but no-one will be impressed by poorly thought through ideas and initiatives, presented simply because you want to be seen as decisive. It is often better to gather information and develop well thought through ideas. Our people, peers and those around us in the organisational hierarchy will notice what we do and what we say. We want to be recognised for thoughtful anecdotes and statements not random ideas.

Really try to achieve a balance between an emphasis on the task (the work) and the team. Getting this right can be tricky. Your team needs to perform but you need to care for and about them too. Being too task orientated will do you no favours; equally trying to be one of the team is a recipe for disaster too. This is quite common if you have been promoted out of the team into the manager's position. You need to work out a balanced approach. And never favour one individual in the team, even if you were/are great friends.

It's always a good idea to treat people courteously, within the team, your boss and your peers; it's particularly important to keep your emotions in check when you feel defensive or angry. For example you need to accept responsibility for the performance of your team. This includes defending them even if things get tough. Giving emotional responses won't get you anywhere and you could be storing up trouble for later. You might not face performance challenges initially but it is likely that you will at some point in this new management role. One of the areas I most frequently get asked to help with is a performance issue of one description or another. Of course, you need to manage performance. It's a really big part of managing people. Even when doing this you need to publicly be presenting yourself as acknowledging that there are issues but state what is being done to put things right, rather than dwell on what is wrong. Clearly personal performance issues are confidential but if team performance is weak in an area you need to be seen to be addressing it. As a leader you need to instil a sense of direction whilst on an individual basis tackling any poor performance. Your actions should be guided by thinking about what your team would say about you when you are not there. Aim for words like: honest, open, performance focussed, reasonable, high expectations, fair, integrity, decency. They are some good ones to have in mind from the word go.

Your new management colleagues

Among those who will be interested in you and your plans are your management colleagues. Within this group you will find yourself in the midst of the organisational politics. This can be an opaque area and take some time to understand. The informal linkages and hierarchies of any organisation are not always apparent at first glance. So this is another area where you need to be thinking about how you come across. There may be some who are your detractors. With these individuals you should use reason to explain your viewpoints. Keeping your self-control is important and logical reasoned discussion should be your aim. It is also important to show that you are not a threat. Keep discussions away from personality. You need to stand up for your team and your objectives, whilst keeping in mind the overarching corporate goals and objectives.

Managing upwards

Your relations with your new manager or director will be very important. Your boss will want you to succeed and to support the departmental and organisational objectives. If your relationships with your boss and colleagues are going well and the team is performing, then that is great news. Life is not always like that though, so a few points here as a way of introduction might help just in case the situation is not going quite as well as it might. If you ever come across bad-mouthing of colleagues do not join in but be prepared to stand-up for your team. If you cannot square that with your own values at least maintain a dignified and diplomatic silence in such areas. Think about how wary colleagues will be to confide in you if you are ready to take part in organisational gossip. You need an open approach from colleagues to make sure that the information you need to perform comes freely to you. Any questions about your integrity will only reduce this flow of information.

Understanding the pressures and demands on your boss will get you a long way forwards. You can use this information to provide the right support and make yourself indispensable to your boss. This is a really good tactic. Always remember this: You want to be seen as an asset not a liability. If you think you might end up in a place where you and your boss are totally at odds, also bear in mind that in these situations 99 times out of a 100, guess who wins? That's right, the boss! You may have very good and solid reasons to hold contrary views and to articulate them. Your responsibility to the organisation and your team demand that you don't shy away from difficult issues, but if you are not able to adapt to the style of management of your boss, then you could find yourself very quickly in an invidious position. If you find yourself constantly in this situation it is really stressful and you might have no option than to keep your CV up to date and make sure that your networking is focussed on finding a new role.

No surprises

One great piece of advice that has stood the test of time is one I received from a Director I once worked for. It was that he wanted no surprises. This means advanced warning of when things are going better or worse than expected. The Director was working at Board level and his own integrity would be called into question if he gave assurances about performance only to find I had some bad news lurking and he didn't know it was coming. It is not confined to bad news though; an unexpectedly good performance he didn't know about could prove an embarrassment if sprung upon the Board. Even risks that you are running should be alerted upwards. That way you can demonstrate what you are doing to prevent them, whilst preparing your boss for the chance that the risk might change from a risk to a reality. All of this points to having an open discussion about priorities and ways of working with your boss early in your new role. Then all you have to do is to keep refreshing that discussion periodically.

You as a new leader

Another important aspect of your new role that you've probably guessed already is that along with "management" comes the expectation of "leadership". You may be one of those whom colleagues identify intuitively as a good leader. You may have shown those skills in previous roles or even outside of work. Defining what leadership actually is has occupied research for years. Throughout history leaders have come and gone and military history is full of stories about great leaders. Management studies have often picked up some of these themes and early theories of management were stuffed full of lessons learned from military leadership and strategy. As you know, **New Manager Secrets** is one of those unusual management books that is not going to be stuffed full of academic theories but gives you proven practical advice in answer to all those 'how to' questions every manager has. So my aim here is to give you some pointers to think about in your new role. As a new manager you might want to exhibit, and be expected to exhibit, leadership.

Some key things to get right from the start

Leadership in your first role from my experience seems to involve a number of things:

Communication of expectations and goals - your people need to know what is expected of them, where the team is going and how it is going to get there. We ask teams in many organisations what they want more of. "Communication" is often in the top three.

Communication of objectives - whilst the end goal may be made clear, short term objectives are needed. Think of these as milestones on the journey if you like.

Lead by example - your own example is important. It sounds clichéd to lead by example, but remember that your colleagues will be looking as much at your behaviour as your results. The way you conduct yourself is important. I've seen the board of a PLC encourage their staff to value each other, work together and pursue common goals, only immediately afterwards to be seen publicly squabbling with each other over resources, forgetting the values they just championed! You can imagine what the staff thought of this... I've also worked in client organisations where I have witnessed managers screaming at their staff. In one company, where I was called in as a trouble shooter, the manager sent such aggressive emails to the staff, we had to bring in a 'yellow card' system. This meant that if the manager communicated aggressively, the staff could email back a yellow card (just like a football referee) which represented: "I'm thinking about this. I'm not emailing back a response just yet as it might escalate the situation further". It was introduced with the CEO's permission of course and it worked wonders by giving people time to think about their communications. Otherwise an immediate emotional response causes a 'defend and attack' spiral and it can really get out of hand.

Support your team - they want to see you are there with them if things are proving challenging. This includes genuinely thanking them when they perform as well as highlighting challenges that might appear. When presenting challenges frame them as goals you are travelling towards rather than simply away from. Instead of saying: "Things are going from bad to worse", say something like: "Things are challenging and here is what we are doing to get from X to Y".

Be tactful and confidential - leaders do sometimes have to keep matters to themselves. You must be seen to be reliable and trusted and that means not leaking confidential information. Don't even drop hints or be indiscreet. No matter how tempting. If you have information you cannot discuss then you mustn't lie as that will undermine your credibility. Simply state that the matter is confidential and that you must respect that confidentiality.

Oh... and have fun too! Don't forget that your people are human beings first and staff second so try and find a way to have fun in what you do. A high performing team can work hard but also have fun doing it.

Developing yourself as a new manager

Part of the attraction to you in this new management role will be the opportunities it presents. There is the challenge of succeeding as a new manager of course. In addition you will probably be looking towards the next promotion. That means that you must not neglect your own development. Reading this book is a great first step! Another fantastic way to do this and to help with the challenges you experience is to get yourself a successful coach or mentor. The two roles are different. A mentor can provide a confidential and trusted sounding board which will help you develop into your new role and they are often people who have had similar roles and been successful in the past. A coach hasn't necessarily performed a similar role to you but has got the skills and experience to help you work out solutions to specific goals and the relationship with them is often shorter than with a mentor, which can be ongoing for years. I've also coached and mentored many managers and senior executives through various challenges in their careers and one common thread is that they value the opportunity to gain a perspective from outside the organisation on the challenges they face in the role.

To continue to develop you might also want to think about developing a skillset as a "reflective practitioner". As we develop in our careers we all gain experience. However, turning that experience into something useful comes from a reflective approach. An experience of a given situation is more use if it is observed, reflected upon and analysed. Developing an internal discipline to analyse the situation, explore what worked and what didn't, consider options and to store up lessons for next time is invaluable. It will give you great insights. When you experience something that appears similar to a problem you have encountered and solved before take a step back and pause to reflect. Don't assume that just because you have seen this before it will need the same treatment as last time. Things aren't always what they seem. Situations may appear similar but can be subtly different. Observe, gather information, analyse, develop options, and weigh them up by looking at the pros and cons of each, before deciding on what to do.

A fantastic way to build on all of this is to join a membership group of like-minded managers outside your organisation. You can gain so much from connecting, sharing and learning from each other.

Your first 100 days

Being a new manager is exciting, challenging and sometimes may be stressful. Think about your first 100 days and what you want to achieve in them. Think about what you want people to say about you to their colleagues; think about what you want your organisation, your boss and team want to say about you. These first 100 days will often set the tone of how you are perceived in the role. You will experience challenges and some of these will be new and sometimes unexpected. Take a tip from the Hitchhikers Guide to the Galaxy: Don't Panic! Panic is an emotion that prevents rational thought. Panic diminishes your analytical functions. You want to run away when you panic. Instead try and focus on a rational, logical approach. Think about the qualities of leadership, the approaches to problem solving and your leadership and management style that I've shared with you in this introductory section. You want to be seen as a cool head with a safe pair of hands. No matter how tough it gets: "panic" should not be in your vocabulary. So leave it behind now as we move on to discover the tips, techniques, know-how, tricks and shortcuts to a whole range of specific management challenges (and opportunities). Remember, **New Manager Secrets** is precisely that. You can read this book in a day and start accelerating your management success immediately by applying these secrets!

Top Ten Takeaways to accelerate success immediately during the 1st 100 days in the new role!

- ✓ Consider "How do I get this group of individuals to work effectively, willingly and consistently, against a back drop of productivity, cost-effectiveness and performance"

- ✓ Keep all the information you gleaned from your recruitment process to help you be clear on your goals, objectives, priorities and tasks and communicate these clearly to the people you manage

- ✓ Ask "why" to give clarity and check understanding but don't overdo it or you'll appear aggressive

- ✓ Remember your team are also a 'social group'. Look for areas of mutual interest, support them and respect confidentiality, and ensure you balance concern for the work with concern for the team

- ✓ Gather information and develop well thought through ideas and proposals and don't respond emotionally if challenged

- ✓ Treat people with respect at all times, with courtesy, openness and integrity

- ✓ Demonstrate that you are not a threat to your new colleagues or your boss

- ✓ Keep discussions away from 'personality' and stand up for your team in an objective way if necessary

- ✓ Make yourself indispensable to your boss by providing the right support, communicating and ensuring there are no surprises

- ✓ Keep your own personal development going, through coaching, mentoring, reflection and networking

Use this table to start implementing:

	Action date	Reflection
Get the group working effectively		
Clarity on my goals, objectives, priorities and tasks and communicate these clearly to the people I manage		
Ask "why" to give clarity and check understanding but don't overdo it or I'll appear aggressive		
Remember my team are also a 'social group'		
Gather information and develop well thought through ideas and proposals and don't respond emotionally if challenged		

	Action date	Reflection
Treat people with respect at all times, with courtesy, openness and integrity		
Demonstrate that I am not a threat to my new colleagues or my boss		
Keep discussions away from 'personality' and stand up for my team in an objective way if necessary		
Make myself indispensable to my boss by providing the right support, communicating and ensuring there are no surprises		
Keep my own personal development going		

MANAGEMENT CHALLENGE NUMBER 2: HOW TO RECRUIT AND SELECT THE BEST PERSON FOR THE JOB

The secrets to shortlisting, interviewing and appointing the best person for the job

One of the problems you face when you write a book is the running order. There's so many options when considering the question "Where does this fit in" and nowhere is this truer than when writing a book on management. There are so many different bits of the puzzle and to be honest there are as many potential running orders as there are challenges. But here's the thing. The one resource organisations and businesses across all sectors need more than anything else and rarely seem to manage to get is outstanding people. Irrespective of the challenges and opportunities currently facing you as a manager and your teams, it's your people who will make all the difference. So even though we've just looked at your first 100 days in the role and your own interview may not seem that long ago, I know from experience that this is the number one priority in the manager's toolkit: to know exactly how to recruit and select the best person for the job. That's why I've chosen to place this as Challenge Number 2 in this book.

Make sure you have the right skills, tools and techniques to appoint the right person

Your reputation may rest on this. Certainly your success as a manager will bear a very close correlation to the quality of the people in your team. So I want to share the absolute must-haves and must-knows about recruitment and interviewing before we go on to explore and reveal all the other secrets to being a successful manager. I often say that I could have retired years ago from my consultancy part of the business if more people knew how to appoint the right person, because I seem to have had so many assignments around "can you come in and sort out the team, the underperformer, the conflict etc!" If you don't appoint the right person you'll be storing up potential headaches and performance management problems for years to come.

No business is immune from recruitment challenges

I've found that no sector is immune from this problem: from luxury fashion houses, large corporates, the NHS, SMEs, entrepreneurs, professional practices like dentistry, chiropractors, accountants and solicitors. You name it. The list is endless. Many managers really struggle when they have to appoint new staff. What's even worse is that many of them don't even realise they are doing it all wrong until it's too late and they wonder why they don't have the right person in their team. It's understandable isn't it because you're often a professional first and foremost, not a manager, and because you are successful in your professional, technical or operational role, whatever that is, you've found yourself either promoted or you've secured the next job elsewhere, in a role with people responsibilities. So it's not surprising that you might struggle with the complexities of recruiting a new team member.

In actual fact this whole book could be focussed just on interviewing! It's that important and there's so much I could cover with you here. You've probably worked out by now that it's a bit of a passion of mine. Recruitment and Selection Interviewing has been one of the most in-demand courses of mine over the last couple of decades. I've written countless articles in professional journals about it and spoken at large conference venues like ExCel London and Manchester Central. So what I want to do in this book is to share with you from my experience what I know are the absolute must-haves and must-dos and later I'll point you in the right direction if you want more on this very important aspect of being a manager.

So here goes! Just like in any other business people are your most important asset. Like any other asset the selection and management of them is crucial. Team members are hugely influential in shaping the culture and success of your organisation and the perceptions and behaviours of clients and customers. So your investment in people is phenomenal. Make the wrong decisions or neglect your investment and your return not only diminishes but your costs could spiral too.

Whether you're experienced at managing people or you're new to it, you're probably finding it a challenge to deal with the day to day management of your team and the communication and performance challenges that some individuals can cause. People can be unpredictable. Some thrive on the current challenges they are facing. Others do their utmost to resist change. Some are so motivated that they will do all they can to remain positive and look for opportunities. Others will delight in putting a proverbial spanner in the works. Some love to learn; others feel unsettled by it. Sounds familiar? Remember, I'll be sharing my proven strategies and tools and give you plenty of practical ideas you can implement immediately in your business to help with all this later in the book.

Avoid making the key mistakes. Read on!

So, as I've inferred, I'm really passionate about avoiding recruitment mistakes because I see daily the effects of poor interview technique and decision making from managers who didn't have the right processes and know-how. Have you ever been taken in by a candidate you interviewed for a job at your organisation? You know the kind of person I mean: Someone who interviews really well but can't then do the job when appointed?

Recruiting employees can be a really risky decision for any business. And of course in any organisation having the wrong person in post can have huge knock-on effects can't it? Get this wrong and you may well experience a host of problems. You risk destabilising a previously cohesive, high performing team, and unless you are familiar with employment legislation, you could end up with all kinds of issues and expenses. It could even bring a small business down.

No-one wants to end up with a problem member of staff so you need to make sure you don't appoint one. It's all too easy though, because the whole recruitment and interviewing process is a tricky one and in my experience few organisations have adequately trained their staff in the key skills, tools and techniques needed.

Remember over recent years people have become much more adept at being interviewed as a job for life is a rarity these days and for many different reasons people are often forced into looking for other jobs or choose to be more mobile than in the past. So, if they become quite skilled at being the candidates, you need to make sure that you as a manager are expert at being the interviewer.

Resist word of mouth

Resist the temptation to rely on 'word of mouth' by the way. This is particularly important for small professional practices where this seems to be quite common and often leads to problems.

I've come across many managers who have appointed friends and relatives of existing team members. I've also seen the many challenges and fall-outs this has caused when managing the team later on. So always resist the temptation to rely solely on word of mouth.

For now, think of it like this. Taking on an employee is just like getting married – get it right and you have a long, strong, rewarding relationship. Get it wrong and you could end up with a lot of hassle, heartache and a costly divorce!

To help you I've selected my secrets to some of the key steps. Ignore them at your peril.

Start at the beginning: Don't jump in. Do a Job Analysis

Enticing though it may seem to jump straight in and think about your advert and the interview questions, resist the temptation or it'll be a disaster. The very first of the 'Must –Dos' is to carry out a job analysis to establish what is really needed now – things change so quickly these days don't they, and what you thought was relevant six months ago could now be out of date. So revisit your business goals, talk to the team and ideally talk to the outgoing postholder (that's what we call an exit interview). Draw up an up to date Job Description which focuses solely on tasks and responsibilities of the job. DO NOT mix this up with the most crucial document of all, the Person Specification.

How to write a great Job Description

So what should go in the job description? Well this document lists all the KEY tasks and responsibilities you want the post holder to carry out. Don't put too many down – about 10 should be enough for most jobs. Write them in an active way, using short sentences and Plain English wherever possible. Don't use lots of internal jargon unless you are confident the applicants will understand – remember for many posts people may apply from different sectors to the one you are currently working in. Do not start adding competences – in terms of the skills, experience etc that's needed – this goes in the next document. Remember the sweep up clause at the end – otherwise you could be storing up problems for later when employees say "That's not in my job description!"   This next point is important: a sweep up clause should not say "Any other duties required" or similar. Here's some more appropriate wording: "To undertake any other duties compatible with the grading of the post". That should help you avoid some issues way down the line.

Probably your most useful tool: The Person Specification

It's all very well to have a job description which lists all the KEY tasks and responsibilities you want the post-holder to carry out but the most important and often most overlooked tool is something quite different. It is the Person Specification that underpins and determines the success of your recruitment process. This crucial document lists the skills, experience, qualifications etc needed to carry out the job description. Don't rely purely on relevant experience. Realise the importance of attitude, willingness to learn, keenness to look at new ideas and openness to change. Attitudes are so much harder to change than skills levels. So you will be disadvantaging yourself and potentially your business if you do not include these. This is particularly important when appointing managers and customer experience staff in my experience. Recognise though that you'll need some really good interview techniques to ascertain attitude. You must avoid making assumptions at all costs.

So I want to stress that your person specification is your separate guiding document which sets out the experience, skills, abilities, behaviours, attitudes and qualifications the post holder will need to perform the role. In my view this is your most important tool as it will guide and inform everything else in the selection process: the advert, the shortlisting, the tests, the interview questions, the decision, the induction, the subsequent training, probation, and ongoing personal development plan and performance management of the new member of staff. It really is invaluable as a tool.

More advanced techniques

Here's some more advanced points to help you further. Do not exaggerate requirements and make sure you are familiar with employment legislation. This will ensure you do not accidentally build in discriminatory criteria that could get you into serious trouble! Ideally, you then want to weight the criteria you are seeking on your person specification – some will be more important to the job than others – and work out how you are going to assess the candidate. You have three main choices for this – from the application form, the interview and testing. Most selection criteria will have a combination of these assessment methods. Draw up a grid for ease of use. Go to www.newmanagersecrets.com/resources for a great example that will help you.

Use a weighting system and numerical scoring system on the Person Specification which will help at shortlisting and decision making after the interviews. Check out the example and see for yourself how this can work at:

www.newmanagersecrets.com/resources

Make sure you do not put in any requirements in your Person Specification that could be viewed as discriminatory and could therefore get you into a lot of hot water, possibly even ending up at an Employment Tribunal.

When stating requirements you must be mindful of the Equality Act 2010. As the Equality and Human Rights Commission says, Equality Law applies:

• Whatever the size of your organisation

• Whatever sector you work in

• Whether you are taking on your 1st or 101st employee

• Whether or not you use any formal processes like application forms, shortlisting or interviewing.

There are 9 protected groups and both direct and indirect discrimination is unlawful. So avoid overestimating the characteristics of the person required to do the job, make sure all requirements are justified and be extremely careful with disability – you have to comply with the duty to make reasonable adjustments. Remember applicants and interviewees, including existing members of staff, have the right to challenge your decisions from both shortlisting and interviewing stages if they feel discriminated against.

Application form rather than CV every time

Unless your HR Department, if you have one, has a different process, always insist on receiving a completed application form rather than a CV. It's hard to shortlist from a pile of CVs as there's no level playing field. It's like comparing oranges and apples. An application form means the organisation decides on the questions it (and you) want answered at application stage and it's a sign of motivation if the applicants are willing to spend time handcrafting their responses rather than relying on standard CVs that they push out to any vacancy they see.

I really strongly recommend that you go through this process with at least one other manager. Working all this out on your own is stressful and leaves you open to potential challenge.

Place the ads, and devise your most important tools – your questions

Once you are clear on the job analysis, the job description, the person specification, and the need to have applications via your own application form rather than CVs (whether online or offline processes are used), the next step to is place your advertisements. Whilst you are waiting for applications to come in, in response, you should be working on your core questions. It's important to devise these questions before you shortlist, otherwise you are prone to bias, by unintentionally slanting your questions towards the applicants who look good on paper.

Questions are key – Here's the rule of 3

Develop a set of core questions which must be posed to each candidate. These come directly from your Person Specification. Then there are the application-specific questions to check out any anomalies, contradictions, or bits missing for example in the individual candidates' applications. These you can obviously only devise once you have shortlisted. Finally, there are probing questions, which are absolutely essential and again you can't really prepare these in advance, although you could easily draft some likely ones. More about these in a moment.

Shortlist using a grid

Once you have written a great advert that realistically describes the vacancy, and you've placed the ad in the right media on or offline, shortlist the applications on the basis of your person specification. A numerical scoring system from 0 – 3 tends to work best. Of course if you have weighted the person specification criteria as I've suggested, you then multiply your 0 -3 score for each piece of relevant evidence the applicant is providing with the weighting factors you identified. Always take notes – just in case your decisions are challenged later. Again, try to avoid doing this on your own – for the same reason and also to check perceptions etc. Most managers work with at least one other in this process – they divide up the applications, shortlist separately, swop over and once they've each looked at all the applications they confer, to check for consistency, fairness and so on.

Why not go to www.newmanagersecrets.com/resources for a great example that will help you.

Once you have shortlisted, notify successful and unsuccessful applicants and plan the interviews. When you are inviting people for interview there is a requirement to ask if they need any special adjustments for the interview/tests.

Tests

Think carefully about tests. There are many types of tests and as many potential slipups. It can be a minefield. If in doubt seek professional advice. Make sure the tests and the language used are appropriate for the role, ensure consistency with test conditions and requirements (taking into account any special adjustments needed by a candidate). Avoid the common trap of taking the candidates on a tour of the office to meet staff and then asking those staff for their views and taking those views into account in your decision-making process, unless they have been trained on your interview process and it has been made clear to the candidates that this tour is part of the selection process.

The interview itself

Remember that the candidates are weighing you and your organisation up as well as vice versa. Ensure that all the meet and greet arrangements work smoothly and give off a good initial impression to the candidates. Avoid what I call the 'Colonel Blimp' approach at interview. Don't use spurious tests or play games to ascertain personality traits of the candidates. Otherwise you are setting yourself up as an amateur errant psychologist and it could get you into trouble. So could playing the good cop/bad cop roles. Avoid all these bad practices at all costs.

The panel approach

Never interview on your own. Work out in advance how you will approach the interview, and ideally use a proper note taking grid. You can access one of these here:

www.newmanagersecrets.com/resources

Don't set up too formal an environment – remember the power comes from your questions, not some bizarre approach using high and low chairs etc. Believe you me I've seen it all!

Have a structure planned out but you will need to be flexible in how you ask your questions so that dialogue flows naturally at interview. Ensure your core and follow-up questions are open, not closed. For more information here check this out:

www.newmanagersecrets.com/resources

Now, there's a really important point coming up. One of the most frequent questions I get asked is this: "how come the person at interview presents like a Mary Poppins: can do; will do; wants to do and then once we appoint them in a couple of months turn into a totally different person: can't do or won't do or doesn't want to". Why is that I get asked. Well here's my gold dust point, so take note! This advice is priceless.

Don't take candidates' initial responses at face value. Drill down using open, probing questions. Failure to do this will ensure the person who presents at interview as the 'Mary Poppins' you desperately seek turns out to be a bitter disappointment!

So if you ask the wrong types of questions you'll get the wrong answers and the wrong person in your team. It's very easy for the candidate to hoodwink you if you ask closed questions (prompting 'yes' or 'no' answers). They may also hoodwink you if you don't probe - asking good open questions (how, what, why, when, who, where) and questions that begin with the use of what we call the 'command', for example: Tell me more, Explain or Describe. Also, using good follow up questions, if you use them skilfully, will enable you to dig deeper and reveal whether the candidate can do, will do and wants to do, (and has done as they claim) or whether they are hoodwinking you.

During my 30 years' experience of training others to interview successfully, I've seen a whole litany of mistakes when it comes to question technique. The problem is that you don't know what you don't know. So it's relatively easy to think you know how to interview – after all we spend our lives asking questions don't we? Unfortunately it's not quite as simple as that!

To give you an idea of some of the problems with questions, here are 7 examples – examples that you must avoid at all costs!

1.   Reading off a script of questions

2.   Asking rhetorical questions

3.   Asking closed questions in inappropriate places

4.   Over-relying on hypothetical questions

5.   Asking marathon questions

6.   Asking discriminatory questions

7.   Asking different questions to different candidates

On the other hand, asking the right questions can have a 'magic wand' effect, enabling you to find out the right information, to the right level and depth, from each candidate in a fair and non-discriminatory way. The trick is to ask the right questions, in the right way, with the right timing, that unearth the answers you need and want, thus revealing evidence about a person's ability to do the job – or otherwise.

So here are 3 more of my top secrets to enable you to do precisely that:

1. Ask one question at a time, a question that is thought out and is designed to get evidence of a requirement on your person specification (remember, you shouldn't interview from a job description)

2. Do not take the candidate's initial answer as read. Use your question technique to drill down beneath the surface, looking for further evidence, examples and substantiation

3. Ask questions that require examples that are behavioural, based on past experience rather than hypothetical or speculative responses.

We all have two ears and one mouth – listen twice as much as you speak.

Make sure you listen actively to what's being said. Remember to show you are listening through positive, open body language as well as your verbal behaviour, and make brief, succinct and legible notes. The interviewing guide sheet works wonders for this. You can get yours free here at: www.newmanagersecrets.com/resources

Decision Making

As with shortlisting make sure you take legible, contemporaneous notes. These will be invaluable for your decision-making. They will also be needed if you choose to give candidates feedback, which legally you don't have to do. Your notes will be invaluable if your decision is challenged and you end up in an Employment Tribunal (worst case scenario). Again, a scoring system can work well. See: www.newmanagersecrets.com/resources

Having an odd number on the interview panel may be helpful for the decision making process.

If you are unsure at the end of the process, it's best to either bring a couple of the best candidates back for a second interview, or start the process again. Time invested upfront could save you many other challenges in the longer term. A 'quick fix' in recruitment is a huge risk – are you prepared to gamble? Remember, you risk destabilising a high performing team. You may have to grapple with underperformance issues and end up with higher training costs. Client/customer engagement could be affected, and team morale could drop. You could even find your decisions challenged and you end up having to tread carefully through a minefield of employment legislation.

Inform unsuccessful candidates of the outcome as well as the one you want to appoint. You don't have to give feedback but if you choose to do so only refer to a candidate's own performance, be objective and helpful – the aim here is not to justify but to help them go on to succeed in their subsequent job hunt.

Remember, if you are unsure, don't appoint.

If you want to make sure you are totally on top of the skills and you are aware of all the pitfalls get your hands on our guide: *What your business should know about interviewing – 76 mistakes to avoid.* You can access it here:

www.newmanagersecrets.com/resources

So there you have it, some awesome skills, techniques, tips and tricks to ensure you avoid some of the difficulties that get in the way of successful interviewing and help you along the path to making some great recruitment decisions.

One word of caution though – everyone in your organisation who may be involved in interviewing needs to know all about this

Let's now spend a couple of minutes thinking about next steps…

Put yourself in the newbie's shoes

Once you have the right person appointed, don't risk losing them in their first few weeks. Showing them to their work area, a quick round robin with the team and pointing out where the loos are is NOT enough to inspire the newbie and help them settle in. And some employers don't even extend these courtesies, believe it or not.

A poor welcome, scant Induction and either leaving the new

employee rudderless or faced with enormous performance expectations in the first few days will guarantee they spend their evenings researching job vacancies again.

So put yourselves in the shoes of that person. How would you like to be treated? What would you need to settle in, start learning the job, and be motivated to want to perform well? After all, that's what you want isn't it? A new member of staff who integrates well and starts delivering, as soon as they are able.

Engage hearts and minds early on

Ensure that you have a great, motivating Induction programme, and I don't mean a boring day when representative line managers drone on about their areas' activities to a group of employees, most of whom have probably been there at least six months – they've probably passed their probationary period by then anyway!

Make sure you offer an innovative Induction, and if your business doesn't have one then create one – for your area of responsibility at least. A blended approach using some or all of the following proven methods can work like a dream: protected time with you as the line manager on day one; lunch with the team; going through a comprehensive checklist with HR – but not all in one go – information overload won't work; assigning a buddy for the first couple of weeks and ensuring that everything the employee needs is available from day one. Not having a computer password, a desk, a chair, the company car etc ready doesn't create the impression of the go ahead professional company you sold to the candidate at interview! Identify gaps in the skills set – there are gaps, even for the most competent of new employees. Jointly set realistic targets, identify training needs, and then create a personal development plan. Enable the employee to network with the key people and teams they will be interacting with, give them a small project that allows them to dip their toes in the water, interact with their team and the broader network. Assign them a coach or mentor, have lots of contact with them yourself – and have regular reviews. We'll come back to this later on in the book.

Ignore probation at your peril

Always, always, always observe your probationary policy and guidelines and adhere to the timescales. They are there for good reasons.

They will help you strengthen a new employee who may be struggling a bit but who with support and training will improve and go on to make a good permanent member of staff.

They will also enable you to make the right decisions, at the right time, if you unfortunately need to part company with an unsatisfactory recruit.

Observing your guidelines can save you a lot of time and potential trouble later.

Top Fifteen Takeaways to accelerate success when preparing for and interviewing for new staff!

- ✓ Work with another manager or senior team member on the whole process –never interview alone
- ✓ Resist jumping in head first - Invest some time in job analysis and planning the whole process
- ✓ Be clear on your up to date job description for the post
- ✓ Devise a person specification – don't muddle this up with the job description, weight all the criteria and work out assessment methods
- ✓ Add to your person specification how you are going to assess

the applicants at shortlisting, and then the candidates at interview. Work out: application, interview, test and which combination works best for each of the criteria you are seeking

✓ Shortlist using a grid, multiplying the scores for the evidence provided by the weighting factors and take notes

✓ Prepare your interview strategy, from the meet and greet to the questions, the running order and decision-making process

✓ Ask far more open than closed questions. You should be talking about 20% of the time – the candidate 80%

✓ Use an interview note taking form

✓ Crucially, make sure you ask a lot of open, probing questions

✓ Remember the Mary Poppins point – dig beneath the surface with those probing questions with some laser sharp precision. Don't be taken in by superficial answers

✓ Don't score the candidates until you've seen them all and try and keep the interviews to one or two days, consecutively is ideal

✓ Don't discriminate and make sure you are au fait with current employment legislation

✓ Appoint the best person for the job – ie the closest match to what you were looking for

✓ Organise a great induction and ensure you use the probationary period to set short term goals, feedback and develop as necessary and don't confirm the appointment if the probationary period is unsatisfactory. Believe it or not, people do and then wonder why they have a problem on their hands

On the page below write your reflections on the actions you need to take the next time you recruit a member of your team:

MANAGEMENT CHALLENGE NUMBER 3: HOW TO START BUILDING A TEAM

The secrets to getting more than the sum of the parts

Few of us would contest the value of teamwork would we? Regardless of sector or type of business most people's roles are demanding. The environment can be challenging, with opportunities and threats at every twist and turn of the working day. So co-operation is vital. A team is not a disparate collection of individuals, but 'a group of people cooperating with each other to work towards achieving an agreed set of aims, objectives or goals'. What I find really interesting is that if you have a high performing, cohesive team, there's so much value add. It's what we call the synergistic characteristics of a team. You actually get more out than the sum of the parts. There's also lots of evidence that points to contributions from such a team being so much better than if the most capable, intelligent team member beavered away on their own.

So how do you achieve this? How do you get your hands on a team like this? Well, you have to build one usually. If you inherit a great team then that's fantastic, but you'll have to work even harder to keep the dynamics stable and cohesive.

You'll need to have an explicit common goal, even a vision and mission or at least aims and objectives. As a manager you also need to be aware of and take into account the individual needs and interests of team members.

But what else do you need to do? Here's some great ideas that you can apply easily, whether you manage a team of one or many.

1. Avoid a mirror image

Avoid the trap that many managers fall into. Don't continually try and appoint people who are like you. Usually a diverse team with different but complementary communication styles, personality types and skills sets works well. Diversity makes good business sense too. So make sure you build all these requirements into your person specification and interviewing processes.

2. Motivation matters

Don't assume that what motivates you and makes you want to come to work in the morning is going to be shared by your team members. Take the time to get to know what their motivators are and where possible use these to 'take your team' with you. Try and do this as soon as you can when you are appointed to the role. We'll be coming back to motivation a bit later in Challenge Number 5.

3. Teams go through different stages of development

A team develops over a period of time and every time you introduce a new team member or change around people's roles, this may temporarily dent progress – teams may need to go back a bit more moving forwards again. So accept this and think about what you can do, and what you need to avoid doing, to ensure as smooth a transition as possible.

4. What's the difference between a group and a team?

A team is bound by a common goal. Make sure yours know and understand theirs.

5. Core Values can be powerful stuff

Run a team event and get everyone involved in identifying core values which represent the culture of the team 'the way we do things around here', emphasising the values and ethos of the way they work, what they value and how they value each other and their clients/customers.

6. Develop a team brand

Once you have got your team core values, you can develop a team brand. This can be a really good idea and from my experience people enjoy an 'away day' approach where they can all get involved.

7. Trust is key

Ensure your management style is fair and equitable. Any perceived inequity in your treatment of team members will be very harmful, motivation will suffer and cliques will form. Remember this: people tend to weigh up their inputs. These are what they perceive to be their personal contributions. They then assess these in comparison to their team members. They do the same with the outputs. If their perception is that they input more but get less out than one or more of their team members, then nothing is more guaranteed to rock the proverbial boat and cause unrest. Unrest could be defined as demotivation, team friction, drop in performance, bullying, lack of cooperation and so on. The list of potential problems is endless. What's really powerful to know is that perception drives behaviour. It does not need to be reality. If a team member perceives a situation, style, treatment etc to be inequitable, it is highly likely to cause problems. Something I frequently hear on courses and when doing consultancy is the expression "It's not fair".

You must be aware of this, and avoid causing this sense of inequity. Nip potential issues in the bud.

8. Communicate! Communicate! Communicate!

The title says it all.

9. Involve your team in decision-making

Lots of research suggests that involvement in decision-making builds motivation, ownership and a sense of empowerment. More heads are usually better than one so neglect the synergistic characteristics of teams at your peril.

10. Do some regular maintenance

Teams are complex machines, so it's not surprising that they need some regular maintenance. Team-building days are a great way of achieving this, provided you are clear on what you want to achieve and communicate these expectations. It's not just a jolly.

Top 7 Takeaways to accelerate success when building your team!

- ✓ Don't just recruit people who are very similar to you. Diversity in the team helps

- ✓ Build a cohesive team with a shared vision, mission, goals, core values and complementary objectives. Why not organise a team day now to work through these and get up and running. Fill out the planner below

- ✓ Ask your team members what motivates them and do your best to create conditions for them to achieve this

- ✓ Be aware that teams go through different stages of development and you need to work hard to build a cohesive, stable environment

- ✓ Share and communicate as much as you can

- ✓ Whenever possible have a collaborative, participative decision making style. Get your team involved in problem solving and having a voice in the decisions that affect them. You could even get them to solve certain problems themselves

- ✓ Above all create a sense of equity not inequity

Team Development Away Day Planner	
Why? Objective(s) of the event	
When?	
Who?	
Where?	
What?	
How?	
Steps to transfer back to work	
Review Date	

MANAGEMENT CHALLENGE NUMBER 4: HOW TO BE THE LEADER

The secrets to being someone others want to work for

The dictionary defines a leader as 'a person who rules, guides or inspires others'. The 'ruling' part of that dictionary definition is probably not what we want these days at work. However, the guiding and inspiring is spot on, and I'd add empowering to that list too.

If you are new to being a manager, you may want to re-read Management Challenge Number 1: Your first line management role and the first 100 days because there is quite a lot to take in and re-reading will help with digesting and implementing.

Whilst there is so much guidance available, often conflicting, on leadership and what makes a good leader in different situations, there is definitely a trend for managers to move towards the consultation or delegation end of the scale these days. 'Hierarchical' and 'dictatorial' is rarely what's required, although it may be relevant at times in the armed forces.

Rather than give you loads of theory here, I want to share my list of top practical tips to help you with how to be a leader at work.

Here's one of my most important top tips to get going:

1. Whatever you do be transparent and trustworthy.

A team that mistrusts their leader will inevitably become a dysfunctional team.

Now for 8 more...

2. Communicate! Communicate! Communicate!

Let's just go back to this point from the previous challenge and take it a bit further because it's so important. Here's a question for you:

Is your team is suffering from Railway Station Syndrome?

This isn't that old story about waiting for a bus, none come and then three come at once. It's not even a story about the joys of commuting; it is something different.

It is essentially a metaphor for forming habits, breaking habits and communicating.

Imagine that you had just moved to a new area and needed to catch the train to go to work. On your first morning at this 'new' station, you observe the other commuters there, noticing that none of them seem to know each other; they don't speak or communicate at all.

On the second day at the same station, you see one or two people who weren't there the day before, along with a couple of others that were. Nobody speaks. Neither do you. The same thing happens on the third, fourth and fifth days and you recognise one person who has been there every day. You wonder if he/she recognises you, though there is no indicator that this is so. Not so much as a 'Good morning'. But then again, you haven't indicated anything, either. Not so much as a 'Good morning'. And it's the weekend now.

On Monday, you go to the same station and that same person is there again – you glance in each other's direction and here's the interesting bit; if you don't speak that day, then you probably never will. It will become a habit to see this person at the same time every day without communicating. Unless something unusual happens. If the train goes straight past without stopping, you might say something. If it stops 100 yards from the station you almost certainly will say something. Something that is not part of the habit has happened and momentarily broken the routine, allowing you to move out of the comfort zone to break the ice.

And much of life is like that – habit. Habits form very quickly and unless we do something to interfere with the useless ones they can blight our lives. And that can apply to our communication patterns too.

So, in the context of leadership, rather than waiting at the station for fate or somebody else to take a hand, communicate. This scenario is really important for you as a leader because it can be used to illustrate what happens to a team without a common goal. The analogy works well. All are waiting for the train here but the goal has not been communicated. Some are going to work, some may be on a social trip. What unites them and starts them communicating is when the train is late or something goes wrong. Then conversation about the goal breaks out, the goal becomes clear to all and for a while there is some unity. Often this takes the form of moaning about the service and how it is making us late!

So, as a leader of a team this syndrome is a fascinating reminder of the need to communicate the team goal(s) regularly. It's so important. I've worked with teams before who tell me their manager never communicates goals, so they all just turn up for work and do what they think they should be doing. Often it's just what they've always done. You know what they say: 'If you always do what you've always done, you'll always get what you've always got'. That's not very helpful in our fast-moving ever-changing world of work these days.

Write down your team goals now:	
When did you last communicate them?	
When do you need to do so again?	
Target date:	
Review:	

3. Do not tarnish everyone with the same brush

One of the greatest bugbears of staff is when their manager addresses the whole team for something that has gone wrong, which may simply be an error by one team member. So, as a general rule, take up issues on a one to one basis and do not send blanket emails or criticism around the whole team.

4. If you do what you've always done, you'll always get what you've always got

We can also avoid this old adage becoming reality by encouraging an element of risk-taking among the team. Define the boundaries if you want, but it can be a great way of moving you, your team and your business out of its comfort zone. Remember, your comfort zone can easily become your danger zone.

5. Respect works both ways

Always show respect for your team members, even if they are not respecting you.

6. Make sure ideas count

Promote and reward creativity and great ideas. Engender this in the way you run your team meetings and recognise that sometimes the best ideas can come from the newest or most junior members of staff. So make it easy for people to feel confident and able to put forward suggestions. Always acknowledge these and, if they are not practicable, explain why.

7. Seek feedback on your own performance as a manager

Ask for feedback on your own performance and build an element of 'upward' feedback into your performance management and appraisal systems.

8. Make development count

Be committed to and show an interest in the development of your team members, not just at appraisal time.

9. Two heads are often better than one in decision-making

Whenever feasible, involve your staff in decisions. Give them the tools, get their input, explain the process and feed back the results.

Top 7 Takeaways to accelerate success as a leader of your team!

- ✓ Be transparent from day 1

- ✓ Communicate team goals clearly and regularly

- ✓ Give feedback positive or negative to individuals, not just a generalised approach to the team

- ✓ Encourage creativity and ideas and give feedback and praise, explaining why something may not work if you can't take it forwards

- ✓ Ask for feedback from your team on how you are doing as their leader and make changes if needs be

- ✓ Have a participative and collaborative approach to your problem solving and decision making processes whenever possible

- ✓ Provide lots of development opportunities for your team members – I've included loads of ideas for this later in the book and most of them don't cost much.

MANAGEMENT CHALLENGE NUMBER 5: HOW TO GET PEOPLE MOTIVATED TO DO WHAT YOU WANT THEM TO DO

The secrets you need to know about motivation – yours and your team's

Although there are so many theories and books about motivation, I think we can summarise motivation in one simple sentence:

Motivation is about the energy and commitment a person dedicates to a task.

So, do you recall what I shared earlier about motivation? Let's recap: If you want to be a good leader you need to know how individuals in your team are motivated. It always amazes me when I ask delegates on a management or leadership course "what motivates your team members?" the vast majority haven't got a clue or are working on hunches or assumptions. This is because they have never asked them. Talking of assumptions, most managers assume that what motivates them to come to work (often money, power, status, achievement) is what motivates their people. Often once they actually pose the question, they find a range of different responses.

Lack of attention to motivation can lead to poor quality work and numerous 'people problems', such as absenteeism, complaints about standards of work, poor timekeeping, resistance to change, interpersonal conflict, low morale, staff turnover, low productivity and apathy. This is just naming a few of the problems!

The managers and professionals I regularly talk to and work with share their people management issues and often top of their dilemmas is this question:

"How can I ensure my team performs consistently and pulls out all the stops when needed?"

In other words how do you get a collection of individuals to all travel in the same direction with you? How can you increase motivation and 'buy-in' to the strategic and operational goals and priorities, have those difficult conversations when needed, manage performance and reduce any conflicts? How do you do this as well as manage your own day job?

So I'm going to unlock for you the 10 secrets of employee motivation to help you build a motivated and high performance team. Then at the end I'll reveal the one thing you must do to make sure that you continue to benefit from positive changes and accelerated success.

Here are the 10 secrets:

1. You cannot really motivate anyone.

Staff need to be motivated themselves. I can't stress enough that you have to find out why your staff come to work. What are their drivers? Not everyone wants more money or a promotion or a career. Don't assume that the things that float your boat work for others. Talk to your individual team members. Ask them what motivates them and wherever possible be flexible and create these conditions for them. People are often motivated by variety, challenge, teamwork, praise, thanks, recognition, feeling important, generating ideas and being listened to. These are what we refer to as intrinsic motivators. They mostly have no costs attached and are about business culture or 'the way we do things around here'.

2. Avoid the demotivators

Perhaps what's even more important than thinking about how to motivate is to realise how easy it is to demotivate people. Look at the above list of intrinsic motivators. Absence of these has adverse effects and can seriously damage performance levels. So think about your management style and see how frequently you may be demotivating others without even realising it.

3. Equity Counts

One of the most powerful motivational theories is that of Equity. In other words we are all driven by the WIIFM syndrome. What's in it for me? If you do not ensure that team members are treated equally you will very rapidly end up with petty jealousies, backstabbing and playground behaviour within your team. I spend a lot of time in organisations sorting out these sorts of problems. They can boil up from under the surface and spill over affecting everyone including clients and customers who can detect the undercurrents.

4. Blend and Balance

Ensure that you have a balance and diversity in your team. You need a blend of personalities, attributes, skills and demographics. There are lots of tools and tests out there on the market to help you check these out and avoid your own assumptions.

5. Dynamics can help or hinder

Remember that when you change the dynamics of the team you may well affect the performance. For example, if a new member of staff joins this can actually unsettle the team for a while and a period of readjustment takes place. If you have a different person chair your team meetings, again you will get a different result as the team members adjust to the style of the chair. This can have a positive or negative effect on motivation and the subsequent performance at both team and individual level.

6. Staff Engagement is vital

Gallup back in 2010 identified that staff with positive attitudes towards their employer were able to share that positivity with customers. It also showed that these employees were the ones with the 'magic sauce'. By this I mean they were willing and able to go that extra mile to give great service and resolve let downs and complaints. That extra mile is often referred to in HR circles as that 'discretionary extra effort'.

So, you need to ensure you engage staff. This includes getting them to buy into the Organisational goals and get them to really understand what they do, why they do it and the implications for when they don't. Set up 'Lunch with' sessions every so often to get teams to know each other better. Involve everyone including the most senior members. It's a great chance to break down barriers. Involve every team member in meetings. Jointly set inspirational and relevant goals and create a focus on and reward for a 'can do' and even more importantly 'will do' attitude.

7. Identify your Champions

Every team has its own internal champions. You know the ones I'm talking about. They embrace new ideas, look for the positives, generally see change as a good thing and are passionate about their own learning. Seek out these team members. They are great at rallying people behind them and become instrumental in helping introduce and embed new ways of working, attitudinal and behavioural changes.

8. Allocation and Delegation – they are not the same thing

Make sure you understand the difference between allocation and delegation. Ensure delegation is an empowering development tool, not an abused time management technique. Maximise resources, minimise slack time and be as fair as you can to ensure you are boosting everyone's skills fairly across the team, taking into account the variables at any one time.

9. One to ones make all the difference

Set aside time each month for a one to one with each member of staff. Stagger these throughout the four weeks and it should not affect work flow or schedules too much. Employees have a right to know how they are doing and most of us relish feedback on performance and the opportunity to learn and improve.

10. Words matter

Think about the words you use. Even a simple "Can you pop in at 4 to see me" can trigger the threat response in one of your staff who will immediately jump to all the wrong conclusions. If you put some context around it, for example "Can you pop in at 4 to see me so we can discuss items for next week's agenda", it makes everything so much clearer and alleviates fear. You are much more likely to build rapport and a successful dialogue.

And finally...

I promised to reveal the one thing you absolutely must do to ensure continued benefits from positive changes:

Changing personal or work habits requires sustained effort for consistent results. Recent research shows we need to embed a new behaviour somewhere between 21 and 66 times before we go on autopilot. So you need to start transferring this learning and implementing this now to start to see the results. The more often you do this the more you will accelerate your performance and the nearer you will get to the so called 'sweetspot' where we have that unconscious use of skill. This of course applies to your team members too.

So don't try to tackle all the above at once. Pick one or two priorities where improvement can really make a difference. Imagine what the changed scenario will look like when you have achieved the goal. Implement them today or tomorrow. That will make it all start to feel real and keep you focussed on progress. Then go on to embed some of the other recommendations I've shared.

So let's recap a bit and turn these secrets into specific ideas and tools for you to apply immediately:

Top 12 Takeaways to accelerate success as leader of a motivated team!

1. What demotivates

Before looking at some of the things you can do to improve motivation, perhaps there are some demotivators that can be removed first? Consider these. Today.

2. Classic demotivators

Consider dissatisfaction with pay and benefits, poor working conditions, poor communication, management by criticism, management by threat, and poor induction. Then add lack of training, unclear standards, unattainable targets, unrealistic deadlines, lack of feedback and lack of a challenge. These are demotivators, to name but a few! Which apply to you? Where can you make positive changes? Today.

3. What motivates?

Find out what motivates individuals within your team. As I said before, ask them. Today.

4. It's not just the money that counts

Don't just consider 'extrinsic' motivators like performance-related pay, other bonuses and of course salary. These often have only short-term motivational effects. Think about this. Today.

5. Strong motivators are often free

Research shows that people are often strongly motivated by a sense of achievement, feeling of belonging, learning new skills, a new challenge, sense of usefulness, respect and personal growth. These have minimal or no costs attached and are often down to your own leadership style and skills. Make some changes and create conditions for these strong motivators. Today.

6. Variety

People often value variety, so look at ways of achieving this and enriching their workload. Today.

7. Autonomy

Let your team members have an element of freedom in determining methods and ways of working. Work out a plan for this. Today.

8. Responsibility

Encourage an element of responsibility in decision-making and problem solving, on an individual and team basis. Progress this. Today.

9. Trust

To be able to help motivate people you must also enable yourself to trust them. Start trusting them. Today.

10. One of the most powerful motivators

Recognition! Consider how you can apply this. Today.

11. Focus first on the things you can do something about.

Make a priority list of actions for all this. Today.

12. It's ultimately down to them

People usually motivate themselves - your job is to create the right conditions. Start creating these. Today.

To help you further here are some thought provoking points to consider. As you'll see, it's often just the mind-set that needs challenging and changing, and increased motivation and amazing results can follow.

- ✓ Successful people fail more often.

- ✓ Does fear of failure get in the way of possibilities in your organisation?

- ✓ Do you reframe failure as a natural result of learning? Or do you give up?

- ✓ People crave feeling special. How do you do this in your business with your team?

- ✓ Are you a member of the I'da club (If I'd have done that....)?

- ✓ A winning attitude can achieve anything. Combine attitude and skill and you have an amazing formula. Is there a need for an attitude change where you work? How are you going to achieve this?

- ✓ Are you creating a culture of positive thinking and belief? If so you should see the skills level rising.

- ✓ Our brain is a staggering piece of kit. Do your employees know how to access the bits they don't habitually use?

- ✓ We CAN change our attitude to a challenge or problem.

- ✓ Do you take time out to look at your business as though it is your first day? By doing so now and again you'll get a fresh perspective on what needs changing.

✓ When considering new ground identify what is the worst that could happen? Understand and protect it – it makes calculating the risks easier.

✓ Do you and your employees ask themselves "What have I done to improve the business this week?"

✓ The good old Pareto Principle – the 80/20 rule. Are you using it to help you cut through the cr**?

✓ How much more potential do you and your team have to unleash?

And finally, for this management challenge here's some self-disclosure:

Whether you would call it a strength or a weakness, motivation and the desire to achieve is paramount for me. Originally built into my business name, it's key to our core process – helping individuals and organisations achieve by releasing their potential to become the best they can be. So, there's myself, my team, my clients, my coachees, my delegates, and of course my kids ....all of whom are the subject of my motivating! It's tiring!

Phew! But let's pause for a moment – what do we actually mean by motivation? Am I kidding myself ...can I actually motivate others or just me? Here's a simple definition of motivation by Wendy Pan, which I can relate to: "To give reason, incentive, enthusiasm, or interest that causes a specific action or certain behaviour".

But where should those reasons, incentives, the enthusiasm or the interest come from? I have designed this book to be practical so **New Manager Secrets** is not the place to critique the various academic theories that have proliferated for decades on motivation – from Herzberg and Maslow to Moss Kanter and beyond.   What is important to stress though is that, from my experience, intrinsic motivators (when we are compelled to do something out of pleasure, importance or desire) are overwhelmingly successful and sustainable in the short and longer term.

Extrinsic motivators (when external factors or other people compel someone to do something) are only of short-term, limiting value, and can rebound with devastating consequences. So BEWARE – leaders, managers and all parents/parental figures if we gravitate towards the stick rather than the carrot. As a parent with talented kids, and more than a penchant for being competitive and driven, I try very hard to heed my own advice. We can guide, support, enthuse, inspire, and lead by example – high challenge, high support maybe – but the essence of motivation must come from within.

Values provide the motivation for us to take action. What are values? We could define them as social, moral and ethical standards, acquired throughout a person's journey through life. These values underlie every decision and chosen course of action. We know that there is a clear correlation between job satisfaction and job performance, and the amount of satisfaction we derive from our work is governed by the extent to which we can act out our values. Often, I unearth employees in client organisations who, outside of work, are running successful micro businesses, or who are high performers in Sport, the Arts or Music. Often their employer does not even know. What a waste! Imagine if the organisation could align corporate, team and individual talents and goals, how staggering the increase in performance would be.

Of course motivation, although it may be the key ingredient, is not enough. To stand out, to differentiate ourselves, to excel at whatever it is we choose to do with our lives also requires talent, skill, the right attitudes, often a helpful dose of luck, and practice. Winston Churchill was renowned for saying "Continuous effort – not strength or intelligence – is the key to unlocking our potential". In the book

"Outliers" author Malcolm Gladwell repeatedly takes 'practice makes perfect' one step further, by stressing the need for 10,000 hours to hone a skill or task to distinction. I have to say it has become something of a mantra in our household, much to the annoyance of our kids, aspiring to success in their respective fields!

So, the moral of my take on motivation, from all my experience is, as Leaders, Managers, Trainers, Coaches, Mentors or even parents, goals we set for others (perhaps because it is secretly our goal) or goals that a person believes they ought to be pursuing, can bring about feelings of obligation, not motivation. Values are human motivators. Allow the individual to connect with their values and to have a say in determining their own goals. Watch motivation, commitment and ownership then increase dramatically. That individual however must remember that if they don't invest very much, then defeat doesn't hurt very much and winning is not very exciting.

How to motivate a team

On the next page there's your team tracker sheet. List your team members there. Jot down your current perceptions about what motivates them at work. Find an opportunity with each individual over the coming week to have a chat, perhaps in a 1:1 and discover what their motivators are. Check what you've found out against your perceptions and work out what actions you could take to more closely align their motivators with what they do and how they work.

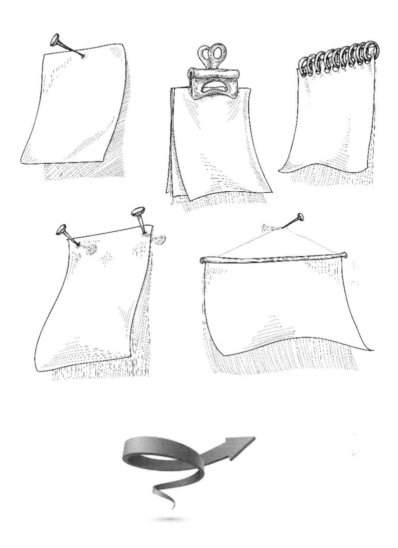

MANAGEMENT CHALLENGE NUMBER 6: HOW TO DELEGATE FOR MAXIMUM RETURN

The secrets to delegating properly

Delegation is a great management tool, but it's often overlooked or done very badly. In either scenario you are missing out on a great opportunity... and so are your team members. Although delegation is often seen as a time management technique, it is actually in reality a development tool. It's a fantastic way to bring on the skills and talents of team members, whilst also enabling you to focus on your key priority areas. This way, others develop their abilities and gain access to more challenging work. You minimise the risk of getting bogged down in low order tasks that really someone else in your team could undertake. As a result, the added bonus is that everyone increases their motivation levels.

Sounds too good to be true? Well, it's an area managers often struggle with – but these essential tips can ensure you master delegation and make a big difference to how you manage your workload. So if you want to know about how to delegate properly read on:

1. Allocation versus Delegation

These two ways of giving out work are very different. Allocation is giving staff the jobs and tasks which are part of their own job description – work that they are contracted to do. It involves allocating fairly and ensuring the smooth running of the team's workload. Delegation is temporarily asking someone to carry out an element of work that is normally yours. So clearly it needs careful handling.

2. Think ahead

Be clear on your objective for delegating and try to ensure that there is mutual benefit – it saves you time and develops the skills base of your team member.

3. Define an acceptable standard

One of the big mistakes managers make with delegating is saying "well, it will be quicker to do it myself" and "they won't do it as well as me". Both of these are usually right – because it's your work. You are used to it and have probably done that sort of work many times before. So of course the performance standard may be lower, it will take them longer and you'll have to explain it all! All you need to do is define an acceptable timeline and performance standard and invest a bit of time upfront. This will bring lots of dividends in the longer term – if the person goes on to repeat the work a few times, they will become expert at it. So you will have up-skilled your staff and freed up time to concentrate on tasks that have a bigger payback for you. Win/Win!

4. Plan

Don't just jump in – plan how you are going to delegate by following these tips.

This involves starting off by choosing the 'right' person

Have some criteria for delegating. You know it's a development tool and can increase motivation. So ask yourself who would benefit by undertaking the task. Consider their current work levels, skills and attitudes. Don't just pick the person who is always willing to help out. This can cause resentment, jealousy and create a dysfunctional inequity in the team.

5. Consult

As it is part of your job that you are delegating, technically the person being asked has the right to say no. So get their buy in by checking that they are willing to undertake the additional work and that they feel confident they will be able to do it with any necessary support, to the necessary standards. If they refuse or seem concerned, it's probably better to ask someone else.

6. Explain

You may be very familiar with the work because it is yours to do! So explain exactly what's required and the importance of successful completion.

7. Give instruction where necessary

You may need to break down the task into chunks and demonstrate how to do the work, or provide backup material/instructions.

8. Agree deadline(s)

Be clear on deadlines that will suit both of you and it's best to build in an interim deadline for a midway review of the task.

9. Check understanding

Remember that the member of staff won't want to look stupid if you ask them if they understand. So avoid closed questions like "Do you understand" or "Are you happy now to do this?" Instead ask good open questions, obliging them to recap to you their understanding of the task. "So, please summarise back to me how you are going to go about this task". That way, you'll both identify any gaps or potential problem areas and can deal with them upfront.

10. Delegate

Once you have delegated the task, remember that there are two other things you may have to delegate. One is responsibility and the other is authority to complete the work. However, there is one thing you can never delegate and that is accountability. You remain accountable for the success of the task, because it is part of your job. So ensure you build in support and checkpoints.

11. Trust

Once you have followed the above guidelines, let the person get on with the work and resist the temptation to look over their shoulder or constantly check up on them. This will waste your time and erode their confidence.

12. Final review session

Once the task is successfully completed, have a debrief session, which will include any key learning points, constructive feedback, praise and thanks. It should then have been a rewarding experience for both of you.

The sock basket scenario

When I'm running management courses and I cover delegation, I usually demonstrate how to do it by using my favourite scenario. The sock basket. In our laundry room at home we have a sock basket – for all odd socks that come out of the washing machine and eventually will need  pairing up. Where does the other sock go? I always have numerous lonely socks that are never reunited by their opposite 'foot'. I think my machine must do something with them. By the way, do you have that problem too?

Now clearly, it's not really cost effective for me to spend 30 minutes or more on the sock basket. But having a university student daughter at home on occasions who may be willing to undertake the task (for a financial reimbursement of course) I decide to delegate the task to her. Now, I know I have to define an acceptable performance standard – men's black work socks are notoriously difficult to match up and my husband wouldn't be too amused if he were sitting in a London business meeting and looked down to see he had one ankle sock on and the other, a long sock, had a big colourful mickey mouse on the outside!

So having defined a performance standard that we could all live with I decide on balance it is worth delegating the sock basket. So I have the conversation with my daughter. Using the above points and the summary Top 9 Takeaways below, script out how the delegation discussion should go and jot the points down in the box provided as a way of practising this all important management skill.

Top 9 takeaways to accelerate success with delegation and a win/win outcome

- ✓ Define an acceptable standard

- ✓ Plan

- ✓ Explain

- ✓ Give instruction where necessary

- ✓ Agree deadline(s)

- ✓ Check understanding

- ✓ Delegate, offer support and build in checkpoints

- ✓ Trust

- ✓ Final review session

	Jot Down Your Points Here
Define an acceptable standard	
Plan	
Explain	
Give instruction where necessary	
Agree deadline(s)	
Check understanding	
Delegate, offer support and build in checkpoints	
Trust	
Final review session	

MANAGEMENT CHALLENGE NUMBER 7: HOW TO RUN GREAT TEAM MEETINGS

The secrets to running meetings people will want to attend

One of the daily gripes I hear when working with clients is around meetings. "Too long" "Too boring" "A distraction from getting the real work done" represent the usual sort of moans. Managers complain about staff not contributing to meetings and actions not being taken afterwards. Run them effectively, however, and meetings can be a fantastic way of communicating and empowering and we know that meetings are a necessary evil of the corporate, business and professional world.

Is it just me or does the relentless meetings schedule feel like it has originated with some thinking that goes along the lines of: if you are feeling lonely, want to use some time up and meet some colleagues you might as well hold a meeting?

If you are questioning the value of your meetings or you don't know how to run one then this is definitely for you. My aim here is to give you some great tips and best practice to help you get real value from your meetings. After all, meetings done well can be extremely productive and accomplish a lot in a limited amount of time; done badly they can waste our most precious resource - time - and can seriously damage morale, motivation and your reputation.

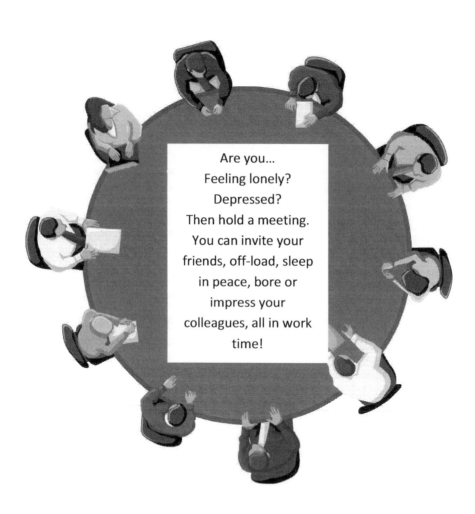

Are you...
Feeling lonely?
Depressed?
Then hold a meeting.
You can invite your friends, off-load, sleep in peace, bore or impress your colleagues, all in work time!

So here's my cheatsheet of the key must haves for highly productive meetings:

1. Is a meeting necessary?

Only hold a meeting because it is needed, not just because "we always have a meeting on Mondays".

2. The Chair really makes a difference

Get a chairperson. It could be you, but before you decide to lead a meeting it is worth thinking about who would be best placed to chair. Ideally you want someone who understands the need for the meeting and what it is aiming to achieve: someone who can focus on the task in hand and with excellent chairing skills. If you are chairing and need to do much of the minute taking as well as the facilitation of the meeting, and be persuasive, well, that's pretty impossible. So someone should chair and another take the minutes. Even if you could perform both those roles adequately it would certainly call your integrity into question when it comes to agreeing the minutes.

3. The people around the table matter too.

Get the attendee list right. Don't simply invite everyone who might have an interest, instead keep the attendance focused. Ask yourself who needs to be there? For each person you invite you should know what they can add. It may help to think that the attendees have to earn their place rather than simply attend because of a certain position they hold.

It is not rocket science and it has been said before, but do create an agenda. What you may not have thought of though is devising an action centred agenda (ACA). An ACA is a road map for the meeting so it needs to be kept to. Don't leave the road map and go into uncharted territory. An ACA will mean you make it clear what the outcome should be for each item – for example use language like 'To decide' or 'To discuss' in your agenda headings. Don't have an agenda that resembles a laundry list with random items as headings and lack of clarity around the direction of travel.

4. Get engagement early on

I've found that sending an agenda round early will help those coming realise that this is being taken seriously, that they need to think about what is to be discussed and will help get every person present focussed around the content. You may even like to issue a draft agenda first, asking for team suggestions. This usually ensures you get engagement early on.

5. Some ground rules

Develop some ground rules for your meetings. Get these agreed at the outset. The ground rules might cover punctuality, contributions, interactions, actions, decision making methods and so on. Getting agreement up front on these can help you deal with any unhelpful behaviour and keep your meetings on target.

6. Timing is everything

It is tempting to simply book slots of time in line with your diary but think first about how long your meeting needs. If it is just 25 minutes then book that time. This will send a positive message out to those attending that this meeting means business and is focussed. You will need to keep your promises, but there is no harm in breaking complex issues into bite sized meetings over a series of time slots rather than one long marathon of a meeting.

Keep the meeting action focussed. You will need to make sure that someone records the agreed action points and when they will be actioned. There is an opportunity to treat each action as a SMART objective to make sure it gets done.

Time limit routine items.

Remember people like belonging to clubs with tough standards so develop a strategy for dealing with those who report no action or progress at the next meeting. After all you don't want to fall into the trap of having a meeting about the last meeting syndrome.

7. How to order the items

Remember, teams take a while to warm up. So place routine items first, put the major decision items in the middle of the meeting, and the least important at the end, when attention spans are waning and some people may have to leave early. You will get much better quality discussions this way.

8. The last image counts

Always finish the meeting on a positive item.

9. Don't have a different minute taker every time

Make sure you don't revolve the minute taker like blackboard monitor in the third year at school! Constantly changing roles unsettles the group dynamics.

10. Make sure you don't just pay attention to agenda items

When chairing, manage the process issues – how well the group is working together at the meeting – as well as the task issues – the agenda items.

11. Use your key interpersonal skills

Use open questions, active listening and don't over control or pretend to have a group discussion when you have already made up your mind up about the solution or decision before the meeting. More about this one later!

12. Manage the three key dimensions

With few exceptions pay equal attention to the task, the team and the individuals within that team when chairing or facilitating a discussion.

13. How to diffuse tense moments

If tensions are running high between a couple of group members, bring in a 'non-combatant' – someone you can rely on to be factual and objective and neutralise the air.

14. What happens at the end?

Get the minutes out as quickly as possible so those with action points against their name can get on with it – you don't want to have to hold another meeting about the previous one to discuss why no progress has been made. A classic!

Start implementing now.

Here are your Top 10 takeaways to accelerate success with meetings!

- Don't have a meeting for the sake of it

- Always have a chairperson

- Invite only the people who have a reason for being there and who can contribute

- Always use an action centred agenda

- Time limit routine items

- Think about the psychology of a meeting and place your items on the agenda strategically for the best possible outcome

- Always finish the meeting on a positive item

- When chairing pay attention to the task (the agenda items) but also the process (how the members are working and communicating with each other)

- Use key interpersonal skills, like listening actively and using open and probing questions, and summarising skills. Oh, and watch your body language too!

- Balance the team, the task and individual, diffuse or manage difficult situations and then get those minutes out on time, using them to prompt actions and outcomes before the next meeting. You don't want to find yourself in the next meeting having a meeting about the previous meeting.

MANAGEMENT CHALLENGE NUMBER 8:
HOW TO PROJECT PERSONAL PRESENCE AND
SUCCEED AT PRESENTATIONS

The secrets that will make all the difference to how you come across

I remember several years ago, when my then 15 year old daughter, chosen to represent her school in an annual debating evening, had to pit her wits against, according to her, the 'cleverest students', all of course 'more clever than her'. The use of every time management technique I know enabled me to slide into my seat at the back, one minute before kick-off time, feeling every inch the errant career mother. Glancing around the room, I felt a pang of jealously for a 'mother and hot apple pie' lifestyle, which would have ensured my seat in the front row. It was only a fleeting regret, but you can imagine my surprise when the first item on the agenda was announced: 'A woman's place is in the home'!

My key area of interest that evening, however, besides supporting my daughter, was not the substance of the debates, but how the youngsters performed. Faced with that many-headed monster, the audience, the debaters' abilities to hold their nerve, embellish their notes, keep their voice under control, marshal their thoughts and arguments, talk to rather than at others and then listen acutely to the opposing side varied tremendously. I read on their faces a range of emotions, from terror to fear to pride. These emotions were juxtaposed in the faces of the audience, the parental figures willing success rather than failure, no doubt taking a share in the responsibility for the outcome. Watching any of my kids perform, and being very competitive, I know I feel such emotions acutely. I actually find it a more stressful experience than any of my own performances.

I admired those debaters. Whilst performances varied considerably, they all saw it through to the bitter end and no doubt went home with a sense of achievement. However, these kids would soon be competing for places at College, University and for jobs. Their personal presence and their ability to present, formally or informally, might well turn out to have been a deciding factor in where they ended up. And once there, how far they got. That evening I found myself sitting there with my people development hat on and could not help but gravitate to those who made their presence felt from the moment they entered the room. They then stood up and inspired confidence in themselves and their views in those crucial initial seconds, and sustained this head start, finishing as strongly as they started, with as much impact and even more respect.

In our working lives, and depending on our interests outside of work, in our personal lives too, our success often relies on our ability to do precisely this. We may be giving formal presentations, chairing meetings, participating in meetings, making an 'elevator pitch', negotiating, selling, managing relationships, or networking. We will be judged. If we get the presence and the presentation wrong, this may eclipse everything else that we have to offer.

Let's return for a moment to our parental figures. Isn't it staggering the influence we can have consciously or otherwise on the development of our children and the young people around us? The more I develop myself, the more acutely aware I am of the legacy I leave for my children. Not in a financial sense, but in 'parental scripting', the indelible marks and mental messages they carry with them through to adulthood. Sometimes I know I get it wrong; in the area of presentation and presence though I know I have succeeded. All three of my children perform confidently in public, actually enjoy being on show, and rise to the challenge. Francesca gave a great performance at the debate, despite losing her notes just beforehand! I have always taught her to have a 'parachute' just in case, and nowhere is that more important that when presenting to others.

I contrast this with a guy I coached this week. He came to me because he had for twenty years feared every time he had to speak in front of others, from the terror that disabled him in his wedding speech to his weekly meetings with his colleagues at work. He wanted to go places, and his fear and lack of skill was holding him back. We traced the roots of this fear to the derision he experienced at school and college, ridiculed for being dyslexic and nervous, by teachers whose roles were to support him.

But of course it's not just about parental scripting is it? It's all about the skills, techniques, short cuts and tricks we can develop as adults. Exactly as I am sharing with you in this book. It's about the preparation, knowing how to prepare, as well as what to prepare, researching the audience, knowing our subject, understanding our physiology and the biochemical reactions when we are under pressure, anxious or filled with fear. It's about being aware of our body and how to make it work for not against us when we are under the spotlight. This will keep our breathing at an optimum level, our voice able to deliver on command, and our body language to become congruent with our verbal message. Recognition of our own personal style is vital too – we can't emulate others and robotic presentations do nothing for the audience.

We can boost our natural dose of ability with a range of skills, tips and techniques. Add to this the belief in our own value and the understanding that we truly need to connect with the person or people we are presenting to and we will find ourselves in a better place. Mentally and physically.

To help you here are some of the tools of my trade, including some secret top tips on giving presentations:

Presence

- ✓ Get there early, talk informally to individuals - you will build up 'IOU's

- ✓ Remember, the loudest noise you will make is before you have even opened your mouth

- ✓ Opening a presentation with impact is critical as we are wired to remember what we see and hear first and last

- ✓ Attention may be drifting, so make the audience sit up and listen

- ✓ Start with one of the following: a question, a bold claim, some news, a quote, a brief personal story, some music, a striking fact or statistic, do something dramatic, get them to do something etc. Choose something that will get your audience thinking "This looks worth staying for."

- ✓ Answer the "So what? Why am I here and what am I going to get out of it?" questions in the audience. Sell the benefits of your presentation early on and give your credentials

- ✓ Share your direction through the presentation – tell them what you are going to tell them

✓ Calm, measured movements show you are confident and in control

✓ Smile, make eye contact

✓ Project positive energy and enthusiasm

✓ Signal you are calm, in control, comfortable in your surroundings and with your subject and equipment

✓ Engage with the audience – don't treat them like opponents

Overcoming Nerves

✓ Avoid coffee and other stimulants beforehand

✓ Never learn off by heart unless you are an actor

✓ Be very familiar and confident with your opening remarks – have some visual aids if you can

✓ Understand your physiology to get your voice and breathing under control

✓ Smile – it relaxes your vocal chords

✓ Use short sentences and watch your pace

✓ Make sure you are grounded – think about how you stand

✓ Relaxation techniques can help – but practice before and find the ones that work for you

✓ Always have a parachute

Talking in front of a large group

✓ Remember it is not a many-headed monster – just a collection of individuals

✓ Organise seating around circular tables – café style – rather than rows

✓ Practise microphones and other technology beforehand

✓ Walk towards and even into the group – don't retreat

Visual Aids

✓ Remember these are to help you and the audience

✓ Restrict content – a picture says 1000 words

✓ Check PowerPoint/KeyNote slides beforehand

✓ Avoid complex animation

✓ Take your own remote mouse

✓ Avoid too much of the 'reveal' method

Answering Questions

✓ Buy yourself some time if necessary – a good way is to summarise or get clarification, even if you do not really need it

✓ Don't motormouth on and deliver another presentation as a response

✓ Give an answer and one piece of support

✓ Build in signalling clues to infer you have more to offer if requested

✓ Never ask if you have answered the question

At Meetings

✓ Think about where to sit – there are strategic places around the table

✓ Don't sit opposite an 'opponent' – sit next to them or one along

✓ Try and speak early on

✓ Ensure you have a good upright posture or your breathing

will be inhibited and your vocal quality may suffer

- ✓ Acknowledge views before disagreeing and identify merit in others' opinions

- ✓ Never say "I hear what you are saying" or "I totally disagree"

- ✓ Avoid the word "but"

Debating

- ✓ Do your research – both sides of the argument

- ✓ Challenge all assumptions – before and during

- ✓ Take key notes to enable logical, accurate and punchy responses

- ✓ Don't draw attention to your notes by pretending they are not there

Your Top takeaways to accelerate success with your presentations!

The top tip is to revisit the list I've just revealed and pick your own top 10. Everyone has their own particular issues with presenting so rather than me prescribe, you need to select those that you believe will make the most difference in the shortest possible time. Write them down in the Accelerator Plan on the next page and give yourself deadlines to implement. If you haven't got a presentation lined up the two best things to do are:

1. Go and seek out an opportunity present – at your own team meeting, at someone else's, at a client organisation or even outside of work

2. Find opportunities to practise some of the key skills above

in less formal settings. You'll be amazed how much progress you can make before you are under the spotlight.

Judging the Public speaking corporate challenge awards with Vince Stevenson, founder of the College of Public Speaking

Alison speaking at a careers convention in Central London

Presentation Success Accelerator Plan	
My strengths when presenting	
My weaknesses when presenting	
The tips and techniques I've selected to build on my strengths	
The tips and techniques I've selected to overcome my weaknesses	
My opportunities to practise these skills:	
Immediately:	
Within the next 3 months:	
Progress:	
Reflection on strengths:	
Reflection on weaknesses:	
Further development:	
Action:	
Dates:	
Review:	

MANAGEMENT CHALLENGE NUMBER 9:
HOW TO COMMUNICATE TO GET PEOPLE ON SIDE

The secrets to communicating successfully at work

Here are some really interesting tips about communicating at work. We usually operate at an 'unconscious use of skill' level when we converse. I've noticed that most of our communication is habitual. That gives us the ability to communicate quickly and saves us having to think too much before we have a conversation with someone else. The conversation tends to just flow and often doesn't leave a lasting impression as we move on to other things. If we want to think about improving communication in the workplace then we may need to change our habits.

Therefore, if we want to improve our communication skills then we do need to think harder about it so we have a conscious use of skill and it's not forgotten by us almost as quickly as we say it. This will give us the opportunity for reflection and if necessary, change.

Use of Language

The problem is that we are often unaware of the words we

actually use and more importantly the effect they have on the receiver. We may live to regret what we've said.

This often occurs in conversations with customers and clients and if we manage staff, then with our team members too. We can say things that we don't mean and we don't even register the potential repercussions.

Here are some negative words and phrases that we can use without realising it. Even if the negative intent is not there, these may elicit negative responses from others or negative feelings which may be bottled up and cause the other person to feel resentful, hurt, anxious or angry towards us. We ourselves may lose out at the time or later as a result. These negative words include:

Always

Never

Constantly

Must

Should

Ought to

Try

Do better

Can't

Won't

Don't

Let's put this into a context.   Words like 'Always, Never, Constantly' used in general statements mean that the person behaves in a certain way without exception. They are words that offer no exceptions to the situation and can create defensiveness in the other person. So for example phrases such as: "You always get these wrong" or "You are always late" or "You constantly interrupt when I am talking" state that the person uses that behaviour as a default.

In reality these are likely to be false; often there are exceptions. Immediately the person you are speaking to hears your phrase they will be thinking of exceptions to the rule that you have laid down. These negative trigger words drive an attack and defend spiral.

If you find yourself saying controlling words such as 'can't, won't, don't' in response to an enquiry they can stifle creativity and motivation. This can then trigger a negative response. To encourage a more creative frame of mind try and reframe these words to find positive reasons to do something and explore options rather than looking for reasons not to do so.

Another set of negative trigger words are words that create the impression that you are bossing someone around. These are words like 'should, must and need to'. If they are used in the wrong context, they too can trigger the wrong response. So if you say for example "You should do this immediately", "You must try to do better in future" and "You need to find a better way of doing that" these are triggers that could cause people to defend against a perceived attack against them.

Another set of words that can sap energy include: 'try, maybe, perhaps'. These communicate doubt and can stifle enthusiasm.

So you can see when communicating at work with staff, colleagues or customers/clients these words are unhelpful. They can attract this 'threat response', usually leading to a negative, defensive or aggressive reaction in the other person. This can in turn lead to a defend/attack spiral.

Instead it's often more helpful to:

- ✓ Build confidence through focussing on positives and what can be achieved, rather than what hasn't been or can't be. If change is what is needed, avoid language which breeds resentment. You want to lower resistance, not increase it.

- ✓ Make sure you give clear instructions, in a helpful, structured, well thought out way that gets results. So many staff suffer from incomplete, inadequate or confusing instructions on tasks. This wastes time, saps energies, duplicates effort and can then even end up as a staff performance issue when the root cause could well have been your inability to clarify exactly what you required.

- ✓ Avoid generalisations and exaggerations. Oh, and put things into a context, avoid innuendos and the potential for misinterpretation and you will get a much better reaction.

So how do you avoid these when your communication may be largely habitual? Self-reflecting is part of the answer. We should be looking for words that encourage and motivate. If we want ideas let's preface a discussion by being really clear that we are calling for ideas. If we hear an option we don't particularly like, we can explore it in more detail rather than dismissing it out of hand.

We can focus on trying to build confidence by tuning our conversations into what can actually be achieved rather than focussing on the negatives.

Negative trigger words can build up resentments in colleagues. They can stifle ideas as our colleagues will be less inclined to offer suggestions if they are constantly knocked back.

Being aware of our use of negative triggers is the first stage of becoming consciously aware of our communications with others, rather than communicating by habit.

Active Listening

This is a crucial skill as a manager. Many people wrongly believe that listening is a passive skill. They think that all they have to do is to maintain eye contact and that's enough to convey that they are listening and interested whilst not necessarily agreeing with what the person is saying. Far from it. Eye contact alone can convey disagreement, disinterest and dislike.

So here are some of things as a manager you need to be doing to show that you are listening in any kind of situation you can imagine:

- Eye contact without staring
- Leaning forwards slightly
- Tilting head slightly
- Nodding
- Verbal nods
- Smiling
- Open posture
- Summarising
- Asking questions, particularly open questions (as illustrated in Management Challenge 2)
- Reflecting back
- Self-disclosure
- Giving free information
- Appropriate tone of voice

How to remember names

Have you ever just come out of a meeting and cannot remember the names of some of the people there?

It can be really frustrating can't it if you meet someone important to you and a few seconds later you cannot remember the name of the person. It can easily happen when you are focussed on what you want to get out of your meeting and the introductions slip by on auto-pilot almost as an unnoticed courtesy at the start of the meeting. You are left then with a problem wondering about how to get yourself out of the situation.

Being given a business card will make your job easy but sometimes if there are a number of people present then the jumble of business cards may mean you cannot tell who is who a few minutes later. If you are sitting round a table then one tip to help with this is to put the business cards down in front of you in the same order that the people are sitting.

If you are one of those people who struggles with remembering names then here's some tips that can help you so that you can easily remember names in future. There are some techniques that will help you put a name to a face and so avoid future embarrassment.

Prepare well and think about the introductions beforehand. Do not slip into autopilot but be ready for this important part of the meeting.

At the point of introduction you need to give the other person your full attention. Think of the name as a gift you are receiving and welcome it. So make eye contact, concentrate and listen carefully. When they say their name try and picture them in your mind's eye and repeat their name in your head to yourself.

It can help a great deal if you notice what they are wearing, what their face looks like, and observe a particular characteristic of the person, perhaps even exaggerating in your mind's eye a feature or something they are wearing. Assigning an image in your mind of something memorable will help, if you in your mind's eye emphasise their characteristics that can aid memory.

The next thing to do is repeat their name back to them in your response. So say something like: "Hi John, I'm Alison, how are you John?"

If you are doing the introductions, then say: "Hi I'm Alison, and you are...?"

Don't hurry through the introductions and if you can write their name down as soon as possible: writing on paper is often the same as writing on your mind.

As the conversation flows make sure you use their name from time to time. Do not overdo this as it can sound false but now and again mentioning them by name will help you remember it. If you did not get their business card then it makes sense to ask for it at the end of the meeting.

Top 11 takeaways to accelerate success with communicating now!

- ✓ Avoid negative words and negative triggers – increase your self-awareness
- ✓ Avoid generalisations and exaggerations
- ✓ Focus on the positives and use positive language.
- ✓ Let's is a great word by the way as it puts you both on the same side
- ✓ Ask open questions
- ✓ Keep your body language open
- ✓ Watch your tone of voice and pace
- ✓ Demonstrate you are actively listening
- ✓ Use nodding and verbal nods
- ✓ Summarise to check understanding and show you are listening
- ✓ When you meet someone repeat their name back to them

What are you going to do to increase your success when communicating? Spend some time completing the table below:

Which are you going to focus on now?
Write these down now:
Revisit this page in a week to chart progress!

MANAGEMENT CHALLENGE NUMBER 10: HOW TO MANAGE YOUR TIME

The secrets to getting more done

Someone once said to me, and I have always remembered it, that daily, time is distributed democratically to all of us. Its inequality only results in how we choose to use it. I think that's absolutely spot on. It's astonishing to think that some people make so much of that resource, sometimes throughout their whole lives, while others squander it and achieve very little. It's personal choice of course, but I know what I'd prefer. Achievement every time!

Whichever type of organisation you work in these days you'll be trying to squeeze more from less. Time is money and chances are there's not enough time in the day. Your work-life balance can suffer and stress increases and your team will undoubtedly feel the strain too. So grab yourself some of these great, proven time management tips and techniques and share them with your team too. I've trained and coached thousands of people over the years on these, so I know they will work for you too.

Remember though with time management it's so important to

recognise your individuality and unique set of circumstances. Time Management is often put over as a rational set of techniques. But we are humans and often irrational and emotionally driven aren't we? So what works for one person won't necessarily suit everyone and as with any skill or approach, these require practice and aren't guaranteed to work every time.

Below is a selection of what I've personally found produces great results at work and/or at home ....most of the time!

So have a look at this list and select for yourself those you feel are more likely to make a big difference for you. And remember! You need to try these and stick to them to get more successful results consistently. Whatever you do, implement and don't give up.

1. A great starting point helps win the race

Be clear on what you have to achieve. Your goals and objectives of your role give you your direction and focus and minimise the risk of being side-tracked. Write them down and keep them close.

2. Have a master list

Have a master list that contains everything you need to do – I include work and personal tasks all in one master list. Then transfer over into weekly or daily lists to suit.

3. Don't work from a master list

It's not enough to have your goals, objectives, and your 'to-dos' on a master list. That simply won't work. I can remember having a manager on my course some years ago who showed me the master list he worked from every day. It had 88 items on it! Can you imagine how demotivating that was – to come into work each day and be confronted with a list that long? Overwhelming and demoralising. To help you work out your tasks and manage your workload daily, you need to have a daily list. Of course you must have a master list of things to do – but don't refer to that all the time or it will overpower you. Invest a couple of minutes every day to do a daily 'to do list'. Only schedule in about 60% of the day, and leave the rest for unexpected issues.

4. Important not just urgent

Make sure you prioritise your tasks. The most common mistake is to prioritise the urgent work. The problem is that urgent does not necessarily mean important. Don't always gravitate towards urgency – remember importance and how stressed you will become once important stuff becomes urgent because you have neglected it. When the important work is also urgent then not only will we feel stressed but we are likely to make mistakes and run round like a headless chicken. So the important tasks that are not (yet!) urgent have to be chipped away at gradually and not neglected.

An important point to remember here, too, is that if you are stressed and short of time your people management will inevitably suffer. So you will become caught in a vicious cycle that you'll find very hard to break out of. I've been called in more times than I care to remember to support managers who have been managing for years like this.

5. Don't polish peanuts

Perfectionism can really sap your energies and your time. Direct your efforts where it counts and don't waste hours on perfectionism if it's not really necessary. This will save you those precious moments for when it really does count. So don't spend hours of potentially productive time striving for perfection in everything. It simply won't give any value-add.

6. Divide and conquer

Use 'chunking' for dividing and conquering those overwhelming tasks on the list. Divide them up into more manageable parts and set dates/deadlines and deliverables for each.

7. Think of your poor memory

Reduce the workload for your memory. Write things down. You get better and more realistic time-estimates when you do, and you will avoid those annoying mental messages your internal chatterbox interrupts you with at just the wrong time.

8. Are you a lark or a nightingale?

Consider your peak energy levels. Try and do the big, important or challenging tasks when you are at your best. Otherwise you will be wasting needless effort and energy at times of the day when concentration comes less easily to you. Remember that your people management tasks are pretty important as well as the professional or operational aspects of your role so pick your best moments to be doing the 'managing' and 'leading' too.

9. Avoid cherry-picking

Chances are that, given a choice, you will always gravitate back to your comfort zone – that could be your operational responsibilities, or the work you find easiest, most interesting or satisfying. But of course this means you could be putting off those more challenging jobs that you find less appealing. Remember, the low hanging fruit we pick doesn't always give us the best results and procrastination is the thief of time as they say! Oh... and widen that comfort zone of yours by becoming more expert at the people management stuff. That's why you bought this book.

10. People count more than time

Be ruthless with time but gracious with people. This means you may need to fine-tune your people skills to deal with those at times challenging conversations, whether it's with your team or your customers/clients.

11. Does speed matter?

Remind yourself that faster isn't always better. This is particularly true when dealing with staff.

12. Eliminate vampires

Invest in doing a time log now and again and check out your time vampires. I guarantee they are bleeding you of your most precious resource. Most of them will be within your control and for those that aren't there are plenty more tips and techniques to help you cope!

13. Batch routine tasks

But remember that people are not routine.

14. Time for yourself – as well as your team

Have self-authorised agendas – book meetings with yourself!

15. Apply the Pareto Principle

The 80/20 rule – have this as your mantra. 20% of your efforts achieves 80% of your rewards. So direct your efforts in the right directions.

16. Staff count, but so do you

Be readily accessible but not all of the time.

Changing Habits

If you think about it you'll realise that the smallest choices you make in your daily life create habits and work patterns. These habits and work patterns form a process and that process affects performance and results. Habits and work patterns have a huge influence on your success at work and on your lifestyle outside of work too. So making some changes to how you organise yourself and manage yourself with respect to the clock is vital to your future success in management roles.

You see, whatever you decide to do today and how you decide to do it will impact tomorrow and probably weeks, months and even years ahead. Pause and consider this: your choices have a significant trajectory into the future.

So it follows that if, using this book, you can identify improvement and development areas and you learn how to do these things differently, better, more quickly and you embed this learning you'll have new habits and work practices. This means different choices, decisions and outcomes to help you upskill, outperform and achieve more personally and professionally. By learning different ways of responding, reacting and performing you make different choices and open up new possibilities.

Let's take time for example. You, me, we all have 24 hours at our disposal daily. Time is the ultimate equaliser, the best resource we have. Do your daily habits and work patterns lead to choices that open up opportunity and increase chances of success or do they lead you into firefighting, stress and potential failure? How much are you making of your free and indentured time?

It really is possible to maximise our use of time, making optimum choices and as result to 10X our performance! Again, this benefits us at work and at play.

Here's something else to consider when you are thinking about becoming more productive, effective and therefore successful:

Who are you distracting at meetings?

You may like to revisit Management Challenge Number 7 on Meetings. Meetings can be a huge timewaster, and here's something that can make this problem even worse. Did you know for example that every time you take a sneak peak at your phone, perhaps to check Twitter, Facebook or even your work emails, you are distracting others who are in the room, even more than distracting yourself?

I was delighted to see recently that the Harvard Business Review is on the same page as me when it comes to identifying the shocking, timewasting mistakes people make at meetings. A study by Harvard academics not only reveals this really interesting point about texting and checking phones during meetings driving others mad; it also claims that checking emails and using social media could in fact be the No.1 reason for unproductive meetings. Worldwide! So it seems that we lose concentration when someone else uses their device but fail to recognise the same behaviour in ourselves.

It's easy to imagine that feeling of annoyance isn't it when others discourteously check their phone, instead of paying attention to what we have to say. We could even find ourselves feeling disempowered, angry and lose confidence in what we are saying. Yet how can we fail to realise that our actions will have same effect on others when we overtly or covertly glance at our mobile devices?

'The myth of multitasking'

Multitasking is a myth. Those naïve enough to believe the hype over the last few years will have worked out by now that it simply does not work. Psychologists and neuroscientists will tell you of course we can all do simple tasks like talking while we are walking, but sadly our brains can't handle conscious multitasking using our prefrontal cortex. Harvard experts tell us that trying to multitask actually takes longer – 50% longer in fact and we'll have 50% more mistakes in the finished result.

So as well as all my other advice on how to have really effective meetings that motivate and achieve great results in the shortest possible time, let's add banning phones from your meetings. If people are bringing phones to your meetings it's probably as a back-up plan. Why do people feel they need a back-up plan? Because they suspect the meeting will be too long, too boring and a distraction from getting the real work done.

If you want to stop your people from losing about 4 working days a month in unproductive meetings then turn your meetings into productive, successful and outcomes-orientated events that people really want to attend and participate in. They won't need a back-up plan then and they'll leave their other work – and their phone – at their desk!

Top 31 takeaways to accelerate success by maximising each moment (at work and home!)

- ✓ Always be clear - at work and at home - on what you want to achieve. Then prioritise
- ✓ Don't always gravitate towards urgency
- ✓ Don't waste hours of productive time striving for

perfection in everything

- ✓ Resist the temptation to continually design and conceptualise. Just do it
- ✓ Reduce the workload for your memory – write things down
- ✓ Have a master list
- ✓ Have a daily 'to do' list with priorities attached
- ✓ Batch routine tasks
- ✓ Be ruthless with time but always gracious with people
- ✓ Really maximise your understanding and usage of all equipment/IT that you have
- ✓ Use 'Chunking' for overwhelming tasks especially and set dates/deadlines/deliverables
- ✓ Be prepared to let go – avoid polishing peanuts
- ✓ Self-authorised agendas – book meetings with yourself!
- ✓ Go by train when you can – you get great uninterrupted time for work or yourself!
- ✓ 80/20 rule – have this as your mantra
- ✓ Consider your peak energy levels – and do your important work then
- ✓ Avoid cherry-picking – at home and work
- ✓ Be readily accessible but not all of the time
- ✓ Update your contact lists, password lists, Christmas and birthday lists really regularly
- ✓ Under-promise and over-deliver
- ✓ Allow a 20 % buffer minimum – at home and at work
- ✓ Have a strategy for your task list stragglers
- ✓ Have a 'folder' of portable tasks
- ✓ ½ hour per week electronic/manual filing
- ✓ Give others early deadlines – but don't tell them
- ✓ Keep your watch fast

- ✓ Clear your desk and at least avoid 'stacked desk' syndrome
- ✓ Have an emergency drawer – at home and work
- ✓ Manage those meetings – revisit Management Challenge Number 7
- ✓ Share these secrets with your team
- ✓ Exercise – I find it boosts energy and is worth getting up early for!

What to do next to take charge of your time

Remember there are

- People who make things happen
- People who watch things happen
- People who wonder about what's happened.

Which one are you?

To make things happen write down the time management secrets that appeal to you and which you feel will help accelerate your success at work.

Add them to the planner opposite. Start implementing right now. Track the results. They really can have a magic wand effect – if you stick with the plan.

Alison Miles-Jenkins

MANAGEMENT CHALLENGE NUMBER 11: HOW TO PERFORMANCE MANAGE

The secrets to getting people to perform well

Performance Management is the term used to describe the continual process of reviewing staff performance. Used effectively, it helps you to optimise the performance of your people; this in turn helps to ensure:

- ✓ Individual success and job satisfaction – yours and theirs
- ✓ Team success
- ✓ Organisational success

So, having a good performance management system in place is so useful as it will bring together for you so many of the elements of successful people management. It begins with the appointment of the right person in post – I've helped you with that under Management Challenge Number 2 – and continues all the way through to exit strategies if necessary. Managing performance is so much more than just having an appraisal system. Here's an overview first of all.

117

1. A great induction makes all the difference

As I explained earlier, put yourself in the shoes of the new member of staff. Remember how it felt to be the newbie on the block? As the manager, you can make a tremendous difference to how quickly the new team member settles in and as a result starts performing well. Ensure that the person is welcomed, introduced, and has all the tools that they need to do their job from day one. Have an 'Induction Checklist', and make sure everything is covered, including Health and Safety and any other legal requirements. Identify any skills gaps, agree a personal development plan (PDP), and set a series of simple goals with the employee. Monitor and review. Remember, employees make up their mind very early on if a job doesn't get off to a good start. The last thing you need to have is a potentially excellent member of staff going home at night googling other job opportunities because they don't feel anyone is helping them to settle in!

2. Probationary period

You'll know from Challenge Number 2 that the probationary period, as agreed in the terms of the contract, is an essential time for you as the manager. Make sure you are setting realistic goals with the new member of staff, reviewing progress regularly and arranging support and training as set out in their personal development plan (PDP). Agree and jointly sign off any additional support necessary and ensure you give constructive feedback. If things are not working out, make sure you follow the probation guidelines for your business and take corrective action, in line with legal requirements. Remember, handle situations appropriately during these initial weeks in case you have to confirm that the employee has not passed their probationary period.

3. How to set goals

Jointly set goals with the new member of staff. These should be SMARTER - specific, measurable, achievable, realistic, time-bound, evaluated and reviewed.

4. Carrying out an appraisal

This is what people most associate with having a performance management system. Here's an overview and I'll give you lots more helpful detail a bit later on.

Use the documentation, the process and timeframes for whatever Appraisal system is used in your organisation and ensure that actions and follow up are agreed and signed. Once the employee has passed their probationary period, you need to carry out regular appraisals with them. Whatever system you use, your attitude and skill in conducting appraisal interviews will be hugely influential in its success or failure. Lots of the skills you used to appoint the staff member will be useful here, as well as your job description and person specification. Review these together, along with other goals set and jointly agree objectives and training for the next period. Allow plenty of time before the review for both of you.

5. Avoid the 'annual rain dance'

Carrying out appraisals once or twice a year does not mean that you don't have to feed back at other times. Don't store up good and bad feedback points. Most employees crave feedback on performance and for this to be meaningful it needs to be constructive and timely.

6. Some golden rules for giving feedback

Comment on the behaviour, not the person. Give balanced feedback, if possible giving something positive at the beginning and the end. The negatives, in the middle, are normally accepted more readily if there is this balance. Own your own feedback using 'I' statements and give the employee an opportunity themselves to identify ways to improve. Remember, the point of feedback is to move forwards, not to constantly look in the rear view mirror. We sometimes refer to it as 'feedforward', for this reason!

7. A powerful plea for praise

One area that staff always identify as a short-coming of their managers is a lack of acknowledgement, reward and praise. So please don't become one of these managers. Never praising staff or saying thank you for a job well done is nothing to be proud of. In fact it can be very damaging to morale and motivation, so recognise these powerful tools and always give praise and thanks where it is due. It's really a magic wand for team building and encouraging high performance working.

8. Become a coach, not a critic

If performance is not quite where you want it, borrow a technique for the coach's toolkit. GROW – in other words, establish a goal, agree the reality and where the shortfall is, generate options together for bridging the gap, and agree a way forward. I'll share more on this later on.

9. Managing poor performance

Workplace counselling techniques can be extremely powerful and avoid a situation escalating. There's some really useful information in one of the later Challenges that I'm going to be revealing on this, so check that out too.

10. Worse case scenarios

Make sure you have robust and up to date grievance and disciplinary processes in your business and know how to use them.

In case you want some more detail, here's some additional information on Appraisal

So, now that you have a bit more of an understanding about what performance management means and constitutes, let's have a closer look at the Appraisal process. I have spent many years working with client organisations and businesses of all shapes and sizes to either implement, improve or provide training for appraisal systems. Appraisal is only one name that is used. Others you may come across include 'Staff Development and Review Scheme', 'Performance Review and Development System' and 'Performance and Development Scheme'. The name usually fits with the culture of the business. Processes, documentation and detail vary. Some of my clients also use online 360 processes to help with gathering feedback for managers and staff on their performance. Of course the whole appraisal system is usually done online these days too.

What all the different variations share though is the underpinning premise that effective performance management is vital to the success of the organisation and to the development of employees as it is they who transform vision, goals and objectives into realities. The 'appraisal' approach is used to provide a working environment and culture that promotes, supports and recognises high performance and individual and team development. It will help align everyone's performance to those business objectives. In short it ensures that everyone is headed in the same direction. It is a reflection of good management style and practices. It will also provide a key tool for personal development planning and identification of training needs. 'Development' is used in the broadest sense and may, but does not necessarily mean, career progression.

In line with best practice many performance appraisal systems do not focus on pay issues. These are dealt with separately; rather, the emphasis is on future achievements and development needs.

Here are some of the benefits

- ✓ Improved staff relationships

- ✓ Agreed focus and understanding of requirements

  - ✓ Clarity on objectives – developmental, improvement or for maintenance (DMI)

- ✓ Enhanced people management skills

- ✓ A forward looking approach

- ✓ Team spirit

- ✓ Opportunity for continued development

Here's a really important point to remember as a manager:

Without regular informal feedback the review is meaningless!!

Any performance review does not take the place of day to day good management practice – it supplements it.

It's a continuous cycle – something that should happen all of the time. The core elements are:

- Establishing Clear Performance Expectations
- Reviewing Performance against Expectations
- Providing Support, Coaching and Development

Establishing Clear Performance Expectations

Establishing crystal clear expectations is the first step in being able to provide effective management support. Whilst the recruitment process provides a foundation for performance, this needs to be reinforced and supplemented with communication on objectives, operating guidelines and working practices.

It is important that you establish clear expectations with anyone who joins the team. Equally, you should check that current staff are aware of expectations and have objectives; if they don't, sit down with them, set the scene now, and, together, agree the way forward.

To ensure that both business and personal objectives will actually be meaningful, it is helpful to apply the acronym 'SMARTER' as a framework to validate them.

S – Specific: Are you clear on the outcome to be achieved?

M – Measurable: In what way will you be able to check the outcome has been achieved?

A – Achievable: It is within the powers of the individual to reach or exceed the goal set.

R – Realistic: Can the objective be achieved given an individual's ability and the circumstances they are working in?

T – Time-framed: Is there a deadline for achievement, or a timescale for review?

E – Evaluated: How well has what was planned been achieved?

R – Reviewed: Did it all go as it should? What lessons could be learnt?

Finally, objectives should be jointly set. This is important because if an objective is set without an employee's involvement, they will be less likely to agree to it, let alone commit to it. By involving them in the objective setting process, you will not only gain their input, but you will encourage them to 'own' their personal development.

Reviewing Performance against Expectations

Performance Management is a live and evolving process, so, having clarified and agreed performance expectations, it is essential you continually review progress with every individual in the team. Effective managers are always on the lookout for opportunities to assess the performance of their team. Note, this is just as much about 'catching people doing things right as well as doing things wrong'.

These are the areas you should focus on:
- Observation and outputs
- 1:1s and interim reviews
- Providing performance feedback

1:1s

Example

Brief discussion on general progress

Note what is going well

Discuss anything not going well/concerns

Agree actions to address concerns

Give feedback from recent observations

Establish what you can do to provide support where appropriate

Confirm next 1:1

Tips for Feedback

For feedback to be effective, apply the following criteria:

Timely

As soon as possible after the event so that it is relevant and meaningful.

Appropriate location

Always give negative feedback in private. Even with praise, it is important to be sensitive to the fact that not everyone enjoys public recognition, so be aware of what suits the individual.

Behaviour not personality

Always base feedback on what people have said and done rather than make sweeping statements about how they are (you behaved aggressively at the meeting versus you are aggressive). Behaviour focused feedback also means that people are able to do something as a result.

Specific

Particular examples which you can describe.

Impact/effect

Focus on the effect someone's actions have on you, others or the situation.

Providing support, coaching and development

Giving regular feedback will ensure that staff know what they are doing well and where they need to develop; but performance management is also about providing the appropriate support so that development happens. The areas you can focus on are:

- General support and encouragement
- Coaching
- Development

Finally, here are some useful tips on running a performance appraisal meeting. (Remember, you must follow your own organisation's approach and guidance)

✓ Prepare for the meeting well in advance

✓ Arrange a mutually convenient time

✓ Allow time

✓ Contribute positively and constructively

✓ Be open and honest

✓ Participate on an adult to adult basis - give free and constructive opinions about yourself and the team

✓ Both parties should agree future objectives and the personal development plan.

✓ Objectives may be maintenance, development or improvement-based

> ✓ If there is any outstanding conflict, resolve this before the meeting

Example

"Talk me through how you feel the last few months have gone in general terms, highlighting your major achievements."

"Tell me how you feel you've progressed in your role over the last few months."

"What do you feel you have done particularly well over the past few months?"

Strengths and Areas for Development

Strengths

In order to encourage motivation, it's important to look at the individual's strengths before moving on to areas for development. Do get them to identify their strengths using questions, for example:

"What do you feel your major strengths are in relation to your role"?

Staff will often be modest about their strong points. In this instance rather than reel off a list which you have prepared, encourage them to think about the issue in more depth, for example:

"Talk me through the areas of your role that you really enjoy and feel you perform well"

Sometimes just a gentle reminder is all that is needed to get someone to talk about their strengths, especially when you have discussed them on previous occasions. For example, if the individual's organisational skills are particularly strong, you may wish to ask, for example:

"How would you rate your organisational skills?"

Areas for development

'Areas for development' can often be an uncomfortable part of the review. After all, no one likes to talk about what they are not good at. Hence the term 'development' rather than 'weaknesses'. Again, you should start by encouraging the individual to identify these areas themselves, for example:

"Now that we have covered your strengths, let's move on to areas for development. In which areas do you feel you need to develop?"

When considering areas for development, it is important that you and the individual concentrate on major areas rather than a whole catalogue of failings. Remember, we can help people to develop skills and behaviours but we cannot change personalities. For example, you may have an individual who feels they need more confidence. If they are, by nature, a shy and uncertain person then you can do little to change that fundamental personality. What you can do is help them to develop their behaviour in certain situations so that they present themselves in a more confident way. So, if you asked them to chair your regular meeting, the process of preparing for and running the meeting with your guidance, feedback and coaching would help them to feel more confident and behave more assertively. Areas for development should always focus on what we have the ability to change i.e. behaviour not personality.

Your discussion on areas for improvement will inevitably lead to talking about how these areas can be developed. Your role as a Manager is of paramount importance here as you are best placed to develop your team. Remember that a training course is only one of many developmental methods: your team may well benefit far more from on the job coaching, sitting with and observing another team member, projects and structured study. Encourage your team to think about these methods of learning and then they can be taken through to the objective setting section. You may also like to check out Challenge Number 14 for more ideas on coaching and informal learning as brilliant ways of developing you and your team.

Individual's feedback to you as the Manager

Hopefully, you will have encouraged feedback on your style and performance continuously. Nevertheless, when appraising managers team members sometimes find this an awkward area to deal with. Feelings amongst the team member can often be "whatever I say could be held against me" and so there is a strong influence for them to 'say what they think you want to hear'. If you find they are reticent about giving you feedback or make non-specific comments such as "you're fine" or "no problem", tell them you can only develop through honest feedback and encourage them to talk by probing. For example:

"How could I support you more?"

"Is there anything I do which makes your job more difficult?"

"Is there anything I could do which would make your job easier?"

Encourage them to support their comments with specific examples and suggestions on how you might address the areas they have raised. This way, they will be able to see that you are genuinely interested in what they have to say and prepared to take action to correct the situation. It will also ensure that the feedback they give is 'realistic'.

Top 10 takeaways to accelerate success through appraisal and 1:1s

✓ Make the most of your organisation's appraisal process

✓ 'Sell' the benefits to your team

✓ Avoid the annual rain dance – carry out regular 1:1s with your team members

✓ Always prepare for these discussions

✓ Set SMARTER goals

✓ Set developmental, maintenance and improvement objectives as appropriate

✓ Give praise and constructive feedback regularly

✓ Be a coach not a critic

✓ Agree clear performance expectations

✓ Ask for upward feedback to help you develop as a manager

Action Point:

Review your organisation's appraisal process. Are you familiar with it? Do you buy into it or are you just paying lip service? Write down now what you can do to improve your skills with appraisals and 1:1 feedback sessions. Note a review of progress date here and stick to it:

MANAGEMENT CHALLENGE NUMBER 12: HOW TO HANDLE UNDERPERFORMANCE

The secrets to nipping poor performance in the bud

One of the most difficult areas for managers to handle is that of how to deal with underperformance. I've found it attracts extremes of behaviour. And like most things in life, extremes are rarely good. Managers feel let down, disappointed, affronted or even outraged when an employee's behaviour and/or performance disappoints. Before they know it they find themselves going through the fight or flight response, our basic physiological response when we feel insecure, anxious, and uncertain, under threat or in extreme situations downright fear. Underperformance threatens the manager because it may highlight weaknesses in their own management style and skills set, as well as the obvious effect on team performance, targets and outputs.

If managers have not been trained in how to deal with underperformance issues their own physiological response may drive them to one of two approaches, neither of which is likely to achieve the desired outcome of improved performance.

They may choose to stick their head in the sand, ignore the signs and signals of underperformance and hope something magical will happen and the underperformance issue will just go away or right itself. There are many risks to this strategy including causing a sense of injustice or inequality in the rest of the team and, should the manager's lack of how to deal with underperformance get worse, an inability to demonstrate that the right support and actions were taken at the right time. This could lead to severe difficulties and unfortunate outcomes should the case end up in an Employment Tribunal.

Equally unhelpful is an aggressive attitude from the manager who resorts to a highly directive, telling stance, in effect bullying, threatening or coercing the employee to 'get their finger out', or 'pull their socks up'. Belittling the employee by berating them in their office, in front of their colleagues or using sarcasm, innuendos and other forms of covert aggression are other common methods managers use when deciding how to deal with underperformance. Risks of a backlash from these behaviours and the fear of a grievance or trip to the tribunal again far outweigh the slim chance of a solution.

So what can you do to improve how managers deal with underperformance? Here are just a few of the approaches we train managers and leaders to use instead of their natural reactions to how to deal with underperformance:

One of the most effective approaches for handling underperformance is to spot it early and nip it in the bud. The best way of doing this is using what I call a counselling skills approach. With this approach I borrow some of the skills and techniques from counselling and apply them to workplace scenarios. In my business I have had a lot of success sharing this powerful approach with clients. In fact, many years ago I had a group I was training on this very subject within the Financial Services arena. It was a two day course and when I walked in to start day one you could have cut the atmosphere with a knife! I was confronted by 12 male middle managers sitting there stony-faced, wondering what this airy-fairy counselling nonsense was all about. Far from daunted I went on to run the workshop and at the end of it there was such a transformation. They all realised that the skills were actually very high level, required some practice but were really very powerful. What pleased me even more was that several years later I ran into one of the guys who had since become a very senior manager. He told me that he had remembered the course and that on reflection it was the most powerful and effective people management course he had ever been on!

So I'm sharing with you here some of the key messages from that course and an introduction to some of the things to think about, to do and to avoid doing, when you have an initial performance problem with one of your team. To do it justice this is an area where you will have more success if you are able to have some face to face training, practice and reflection, but having said that it's still valuable to share it here to give you some initial insights and ideas for a way forward.

Consider this: Did you know that most managers are more likely to talk about a performance or conduct issue concerning a member of staff to everyone else but that person?

Of course it can often be difficult can't it to decide whether a person's poor performance should be handled as a conduct or capability issue. In some cases, a problem may appear at first to be a conduct issue, but later turns out to be one of capability or vice versa. It could even be a combination of both.

The question though is this:

Why is it that managers find addressing initial concerns about underperformance with the said team member so hard?

And what's more:

Why is it that managers' styles seem to veer to one extreme or the other?

On the one hand managers will stick their head in the sand and avoid that initial conversation to demonstrate that they've picked up some worrying signs or they go to the other extreme and call a meeting, all gung-ho and guns blazing, determined to tear the person off a strip and tell them what's what!

Of course there are various shades in the middle too. These include:

- Dropping hints
- Innuendos
- Inferences
- Extolling the virtues of other team members in the hope that these rub off
- Bullying
- Sarcasm

Ever worry it may affect your own performance?

One of the managers I've been coaching recently said to me "Performance issues are ruling my life. Joe Bloggs is showing signs of demotivation and their time-keeping and output have really deteriorated. I can't quite put my finger on why, but I spend more time worrying about that than focussing on the rest of my team. I'm even worrying now that it'll affect my own performance."

What might we mean by underperformance?

It's useful to explore what we mean by underperformance.

Here are some popular definitions:

- To fail to do as well as expected
- To exhibit a level of performance that is below standard
- To perform less well than others
- To perform less well than expected

Detecting it early on

Here are just a few of the signs and symptoms of a potential performance problem:

- A shift in behaviour downwards - consistently performing below expectations when previously performance was adequate or more
- Poor customer care
- Lack of attention to detail
- Persistent errors
- Rudeness
- Argumentative
- Causing unnecessary friction
- Not listening
- Arriving late
- Poor timekeeping for meetings and other events
- Monday/Friday pattern in absence

- ➤ Bullying or sarcastic behaviour

- ➤ Withdrawal

- ➤ Disrespectful to you or colleagues

- ➤ Lack of willingness to take on extra duties

- ➤ Other visible changes to normal behaviour patterns

Remember it is important to establish if it is down to conduct or capability and to recognise it may be a combination of both. Sometimes as a manager it seems as though it is a conduct issue and then turns out to be capability or vice versa.

Here are a couple of examples:

Under-performance as a result of conduct may include:

- ➤ Persistently turning up late

- ➤ Failure to follow clear and reasonable instructions

- ➤ Bullying other team members

Examples of under-performance as a result of capability may include:

- ➤ Poor communication skills with customers/clients

- ➤ Lack of interpersonal skills with colleagues

- ➤ Length of time to complete tasks

- ➤ Repeated errors

Common assumptions about why there's underperformance

It's very easy as the manager to make assumptions as to why there is now a problem. The most common assumptions seem to be:

> ➤ The team member has turned into a poor appointment

> ➤ The team member is being influenced negatively by others in the team

> ➤ The team member is lazy

> ➤ The team member is careless

> ➤ The team member obviously can't cope

> ➤ The team member must have problems outside of work

So assumptions are often made about the cause of a dip in performance, negative shift in motivation, change in attitude, friction with others, time-keeping etc. Sometimes the assumption may be right, but often it is not the case.

Would you consider that you could be partially responsible?

Here are some potential causes that actually say more about the manager's performance than that of the team member:

> ➤ It was a poor appointment in the first place

> ➤ Inadequate induction

> ➤ Poorly managed probationary period

> ➤ Probation was signed off successfully despite contra-indicators

> ➤ Lack of instruction

> ➤ Inappropriate delegation

> ➤ Poor work scheduling

> ➤ Poor allocation of work

> ➤ Lack of resources

> ➤ IT/equipment and other tools not working effectively

- ➢ Confusion or lack of clarity over goals
- ➢ Inappropriate objectives
- ➢ Lack of reward systems
- ➢ Ineffective procedures
- ➢ Lack of feedback
- ➢ Lack of support
- ➢ Perceived inequity
- ➢ Leadership or management style
- ➢ No variation/job enrichment/job rotation

The learning point here is this. It's always useful to look to yourself first of all. Have you as the manager unwittingly caused or exacerbated the issue?

Here are examples of causes associated with the team member:

- ➢ Illness
- ➢ Medication
- ➢ Poor choice of role/job
- ➢ Stress – from work or home life
- ➢ Inability to cope with change
- ➢ Difficult relationships with other colleagues
- ➢ Mindset issues/low self-esteem
- ➢ Capability
- ➢ Problems with work/life balance
- ➢ Restrictive comfort zone

Why usual management approaches may be unhelpful

Habitual management responses may be the opposite of what's needed initially to resolve the problem. Managers are of course trained to identify problems, generate solutions, take decisions and solve the problem. Unfortunately in the case of initial underperformance this approach can be really unhelpful and actually lead to an inappropriate solution that does not have the buy-in from the employee, and at best may become a temporary sticking plaster whilst the root cause of the problem remains undiscovered. So some of the usual skills and tools in the manager's tool kit can actually become a disadvantage when trying to have an initial performance discussion.

Ever taken it personally?

Another factor that can get in the way of the manager being well placed to nip a performance issue in the bud is that they can take it personally. They may perceive the underperformance as deliberate and as an insult. In other words they may take it personally. This means that the way they approach the initial performance conversation is emotionally driven, often leading them into aggressive or emotive language. From an expectation management perspective the manager often approaches the discussion in the belief that the team member will open up and share. This may well not happen. Equally false beliefs may include "If I tell them they've got to change they will if they value their job" and "If I am nice and point out how disappointed I am and then give them a solution it will all be fine".

Ever made these mistakes when tackling the first signs of a performance problem?

Before going on to look at some solutions, here's a list of the most common pitfalls which managers fall into when there are the first signs of a performance issue:

- ✘ Talk to others first rather than the person
- ✘ Put it off
- ✘ Tackle it head on without the right planning and often communicate aggressively
- ✘ Not listening
- ✘ Inappropriate seating arrangements
- ✘ Poor body language
- ✘ Creating a formal or tense environment – or both
- ✘ Asking all the wrong questions
- ✘ Talking about 'evidence'
- ✘ Mentioning others by name
- ✘ Going on hearsay
- ✘ Taking lots of notes
- ✘ Talking most of the time
- ✘ Making assumptions
- ✘ Jumping in too early with a conclusion
- ✘ Threatening formal procedures when that isn't appropriate or necessary
- ✘ Rushing too quickly to a solution
- ✘ Being too soft and taking on too much responsibility for the situation themselves
- ✘ Being too judgemental
- ✘ Unable to suspend judgement
- ✘ Continuing to move forward on assumptions
- ✘ Solving the problem themselves

✘   Not building in and diarising firm follow ups to check progress

How to address the problem early on and use some powerful skills for early resolution

Feeling equipped as a manager to tackle performance challenges clearly has many benefits. One of the crucial 'must-haves' is to learn the skills, techniques and confidence to prevent situations escalating into full blown performance management challenges which can be very costly and time-consuming. Another is to develop skills and techniques to motivate and inspire performance and team work and equip key staff to handle signs and symptoms of problems.

By acquiring the skills to handle a variety of situations with staff in a sensitive, caring and yet powerful way means that you are less likely to have serious issues and should they occur, you will be able to demonstrate as a good employer you have done everything you can to try and resolve them.

Here's what every manager needs to know and be able to achieve when working with potential performance issues:

How to:

✓ Use a 'counselling approach' to identify and acknowledge issues

✓ Rethink and redefine habitual responses to people problems and performance issues

✓ Use these techniques to support the individual to find solutions to maximise performance

✓ Gain powerful tools which may well prevent issues escalating to disciplinary/conduct and capability routes

Here's some guidelines to help you think about how to run a counselling approach to solve these initial performance problems. I hope this helps but you do need to attend training to be able to do this well.

- ✓ Set up a non-threatening environment for a private 1:1 conversation

- ✓ Do not adopt a submissive or aggressive approach

- ✓ Increase awareness of and use more consciously the 5 listening styles of EISPU (you need training for this)

- ✓ Master question technique, including the adept use of open questions and useful deflections

- ✓ Use collaborative rather than combative language, which to some may seem counter-intuitive when working out how to deal with underperformance.

- ✓ Transition from a directive style to an enabling style which involves the underperforming employee determining the solution. Consider what is appropriate and what you need to do to progress the solution

- ✓ Avoid assumptions

- ✓ Seek the employee's view first

- ✓ Be fair, flexible but also firm when necessary and don't allow yourself to be side-tracked

- ✓ Agree what the change will look like and what needs to happen to secure this

- ✓ Set a review date and ensure the follow up to check that the agreed action on to how to deal with underperformance issues is working

- ✓ Measure and monitor

✓ If the change does not happen or does not stick escalate as appropriate

So the whole issue of managing underperformance is a really important challenge to be aware of. Let's say it's been an eye opener and you have started to think about how the early warning signs of performance issues are recognised and handled by the managers in your organisation. A performance counselling approach can save you time, money and considerable aggravation, stress and even litigation. Always consult with your HR department if you have one, or seek legal advice if you are unsure. I'm not going to deal with Grievance and Disciplinary processes and other specific employment issues in this book. It's complex and outside the remit of **New Manager Secrets.**

Top 10 takeaways to accelerate your success and that of your team member when managing underperformance

- ✓ Don't stick your head in the sand and ignore the signs
- ✓ Don't use a bullying, aggressive approach
- ✓ Detect it early on and nip it in the bud
- ✓ Use a counselling skills approach
- ✓ Consider if it is conduct or capability or both
- ✓ Check it's not your fault
- ✓ Don't take it personally
- ✓ Transition from a directive style to an enabling style
- ✓ Seek Human Resources and/or legal advice if necessary re: disciplinary, grievance and other procedures
- ✓ Go get some training in how to use the skills to carry out this counselling skills approach

MANAGEMENT CHALLENGE NUMBER 13: HOW TO HANDLE DIFFICULT PEOPLE AND CONFLICT

The secrets to resolving difficulties and conflict

What do you do if two members of your staff are not getting on?

It's an inevitable risk in working life that there will at times be conflict between two or more of your team members. It's so important that you aim for an early resolution, as the conflict could escalate and cause no end of problems for you.

Your goal should be to reach a win/win situation where the individuals go back to giving their best at work, with their energies no longer being diverted from their priorities and tasks.

Ever heard of the Persian poet Rumi?

"Out beyond ideas of wrong doing and right doing there is a field. I'll meet you there".

This insightful poet, **800 years ago,** was encouraging us to look beyond the immediacy of turmoil and conflict, to greener pastures rich with possibilities for resolution and solution. This fits rather well with the theme of the cost of conflict in the workplace and the potential tools for collaboration and harmony.

How far do you think we have come in the last 800 years? How well placed are we as human beings to be emotionally intelligent, to 'engage brain before opening mouth and inserting foot'? What happens in demanding situations where we may feel threatened by someone with a different viewpoint, or whom we perceive is seeking to achieve something at our expense or the expense of others? How able are we to resist the power of our reptilian brain which can instantaneously trigger our fight or flight response, emotions getting in the way and propelling us into aggression or submission?

As a manager you need to be aware of the cost of conflict and know how to avoid it, minimise or worse case deal with it. Numerous reports in professional journals scream headlines like:

"Poor conflict management skills cost UK plcs billions"

And

"Conflict costs UK businesses £24 billion every year due to lost working days, with an average worker spending at least 2 hours a week dealing with conflict"

Exactly how many lost working days was that due to conflict?

370 million. Annually. In the UK. Alone.

From my experience personality clashes and 'warring egos' are found to be the primary cause for conflict. I would also acknowledge stress and heavy workloads as contributory factors. In one of my client organisations I would estimate that 2 hours a day were lost due to the effect of having to sort out conflict! Conflict can occur in any type of team or organisation. It can be particularly damaging in smaller businesses like professional practices because it is harder to conceal it and easier to reveal it to clients, customers, patients etc. And of course in smaller businesses you'll be less likely to easily access professional advice and support.

According to research, causal factors include those all too common personality clashes, taking credit for others' ideas and work, talking over people in badly run meetings, talking behind people's backs, ignoring colleagues, personal remarks, relentless criticism, bullying, harassment, low morale and absence. Insidious, covert aggression within the workplace causes untold damage.

Some of the recent statistics I checked out point to in excess of 12 days a year per 100 employees being spent by HR and management in managing grievance and disciplinary cases. A naive and optimistic view might be that after years of recession, we would be thankful to be at work, would adopt a caring and collaborative way of working, and at least temporarily be prepared to forego the game-playing that so often wounds the colleague and maims the organisation. Not so, according to the evidence.

Let's not forget that there are positive outcomes to conflict, with possibilities including recognition of and valuing differences, dusting down complacency, releasing energy and increasing commitment. There is a greater chance of future collaborative working and breakthroughs in thinking if we have the appropriate tools to understand and resolve conflict. The reality is that often we do not, and the risks attached range from anger, misery and a phenomenal amount of wasted energy, to bad, sometimes disastrous, decisions, demotivation, resistance and downright sabotage. At the very least you will have absence rates that will affect your bottom line/value for money.

So, as leaders and managers, where should we be turning our attention in the war against conflict?

The tips below are just a few of the many things you can do to find effective and productive ways forward.

To minimise risk of conflict:

- Walk the talk. Don't just say you value your staff. Ensure you do and demonstrate it.

- Invest in tools and interventions that help people become more emotionally intelligent, self-aware, and assertive rather than aggressive. This can include assertiveness training, coaching and confidence building, team events and development days

- Have regard for the 'psychological' contract with employees

- Don't go overdrawn at the employee's 'emotional bank account'[2]

- Remember that 'Intention' and 'Impact' are different things

- There is no reality – only perception – ensure there is respect for each individual's unique map of the world – how they see things, values, belief systems etc.

- Communication is key. Consider what works best and when, based on the goal. Issues that can impact include language and diversity, frequency, time available, transparency, effectiveness, Visual, Auditory and Kinaesthetic (VAK) channels which indicate people's communication style preferences and organisational culture

- Be aware of the iceberg effect – visible symptoms and potential underlying causes may not be the same when it

---

[2] Stephen R Covey

comes to disagreements, clashes and relationship breakdowns.

Here are some other practical actions you can take as the manager to manage conflict:

1. Find out the root cause

Consider what is getting in the way of an effective working relationship. There could be a number of causes including vested interests, change, jealousy, personality clashes, power struggles, miscommunication or insecurities.

2. Have you contributed to the problem?

Check that you have not been inequitable in your management of the individuals concerned.

However much you plan, you can often receive the one response you hadn't catered for. I've already identified some words that are likely to cause people to become defensive and feel under attack in Management Challenge Number 9. Put yourself in that situation for a moment. When we feel like that we often become more difficult to deal with. For example we may:

- Interrupt
- Raise our voice
- Refuse to listen
- Close our body language
- Close our mind
- Open our mouth and insert foot!

If you find yourself dealing with someone who is reacting negatively, even if you yourself have at least partially caused the situation by how you handled the issue, what can you do when faced with this style of reaction?

Here are some ideas:

> Try to avoid debating the issue. This fuels any disagreement already present because the other person will always try to justify their position from their standpoint. You will end up sounding defensive too. The situation may escalate, tempers flare and a solution remains out of reach.

> Don't give up though. If you do this encourages them to continue to use a behavioural style which gets their own way. Agreement will never be reached and the other person will always use the learned behaviour that gets what they want.

> Use your key interpersonal şkills. Show you understand their position. Listen actively. Gain a thorough understanding of their point of view. Use reflecting, paraphrasing and summarising skills, you don't have to agree with them, you just have to understand them.

> Use your question technique to clarify and seek understanding rather than using strategies to counter-attack.

> Stick to facts not opinions and state your position. Facts can be justified and shouldn't be seen as blame and personal attacks.

> Be positive in your language and intentions. State intended positive outcomes. Create a sense of both moving forward in the right direction towards a solution.

> Then work on a mutually acceptable resolution together.

> ➤ As they say, communication is key.

3. No one reality

Remember, there is often no 'right' or 'wrong'. Perception drives behaviour and perceptual differences can be very powerful. We see the world through different lenses and depending which 'glasses' you are wearing, you will see different things. Try hard to see and respect different viewpoints. This means suspending judgement, asking a bunch of open questions, really actively listening, summarising, reflecting back and remaining objective.

4. Consider the level of current conflict

What's happening currently? Is it irritation? Annoyance? Anger? Or worst case – verbal or even physical 'violence'?

5. Use GROW

Try using the GROW Coaching model with each person – Goals, Reality, Options, Way Forward. For more material here check out: www.newmanagersecrets/resources

6. Identify individuals' views

Sit down with each individual. Help them identify the true source. You may need to challenge generalisations, assumptions and any sweeping statements. Ask for specific examples and check these out.

7. Get another perspective

Help the individuals to understand the situation from some-one else's perspective.

8. Establish the cost of conflict

Discuss with each individual the cost of conflict and what will happen if the situation does not change.

9. Remain neutral

Be unbiased and show no favouritism.

10. Workplace counselling skills approaches may help

You could also check out the advice I gave in the workplace counselling skills section on the previous Management Challenge (Number 12). Why not reread that and see if some of it will help with the conflict situation you may be experiencing.

11. Consider a mediator

If your efforts don't work, consider contacting HR, specialist advice or bringing in a trained mediator.

So to summarise

- Identify, address and seek to resolve conflict at as low a level as possible. It's likely to escalate otherwise.

- When dealing with conflict between two parties, see them individually first.

- Have a toolbox of approaches including diffusion techniques and assertive and negotiating skills.

- Remember! There is a range of coaching models and techniques to effectively coach around conflict issues.

Finally, returning to Jalal ad-Din Muhammad Rumi, our poet, leave the accusations, positions and protracted arguments behind. Search together for common ground and focus on the way forward:

"Since in order to speak, one must first listen, learn to speak by listening" Rumi

Top 15 takeaways to accelerate your success when dealing with conflict issues

- ✓ Walk the talk. Don't just say you value your staff. Ensure you do and demonstrate it

- ✓ Invest in tools and interventions that help people become more emotionally intelligent

- ✓ Have regard for the 'psychological' contract with employees

- ✓ Don't go overdrawn at the employee's 'emotional bank account'

- ✓ Remember that 'Intention' and 'Impact' are different things

- ✓ There is no one reality

- ✓ Communication is key. Consider what works best and when, based on the goal

- ✓ Be aware of the iceberg effect and find out the root cause

- ✓ Try to avoid debating the issue

- ✓ Don't give up though

- ✓ Use your key interpersonal skills

- ✓ Use your question technique to clarify and seek understanding

- ✓ Stick to facts not opinions and state your position

- ✓ Be positive in your language and intentions

- ✓ Work on a mutually acceptable resolution together

Action Point: Pick 3 of the strategies from the previous page and keep them up your sleeve, just in case you need them.

1.

2.

3.

MANAGEMENT CHALLENGE NUMBER 14: HOW TO DEVELOP YOUR TEAM

The secrets to fast-tracking your people's development

I got into the people development space very early on, in the 1980s, and at that time I think it's fair to say that there were minimal opportunities for training and development. It's now a multi-billion dollar industry. How does this help you? Well, there are so many opportunities, alternatives and technologies to support your own personal development and that of the people you manage.

So that's great news. Again, this whole book could just be on people development opportunities. What I want to do here, though, is simply give you an overview of just some of the options, focussing on learning within your workplace, and in particular, how you as a manager can develop your people.

Why is this so important? People are your most important asset as a manager. We've all heard that said many times before, haven't we? But despite all the opportunities it's often rhetoric and goes no further in organisations than the annual report, the job advert, and the glossy client literature. At best, it may reach the lips of managers

155

– but that's usually firmly where it stays. It's often the case that professional and operational training takes priority which is understandable but there needs to be a more holistic approach. It seems to me sometimes there's a disconnect between HR, Learning and Development teams, the raft of opportunities for training, learning and development, and managers at the coal face.

The managers and staff I regularly talk to tell me it feels as though they are having to cope with new challenges and changes on an almost daily basis. I don't think that is going to change. As I said early on in this book, there's a continual drive towards efficiencies and effectiveness, and you've got to be smarter than your competitors. Organisations have to give value-add constantly, not only to customers, clients, or patients, but also to their staff. As a manager you need to lead and manage change, to engage and empower the people who work with you. Staff need to be able to invent, to innovate and work smarter too. This all requires upskilling and maximising behaviours at work. And of course, because of the pace of change, learning and improvement needs to be continuous too. Does this sound familiar to you? And of course it's not just money that needs to be found for development. From my experience with clients, time has overtaken budgets as the most precious resource.

Clients tell me that their most preferred way of upskilling their staff used to be to send them on courses, preferably bespoked in house, but also external, depending on needs. I think courses are great too – we've won awards for ours! But we know that courses alone, however good, are no longer the panacea. Current challenges require additional, powerful learning solutions, preferably ones that don't take people 'away from the ranch' for too long. If people can continue to work whilst learning so much the better.

So to solve this particular management challenge, here are some ideas that you can work through and choose from.

Coaching conversations and how to do it

Firstly, let's pick up on the idea of coaching conversations, which I mentioned in Management Challenge Number 11: How to performance manage.

At times you will be looking to engage to a greater level with your staff, seeking to support them with growth in their performance and career ambitions, to instigate better working relationships amongst team members and ultimately to improve your own and organisational success.

As a manager you will be talking with your employees regularly on various aspects of the organisation, the business priorities, outputs and their roles within it. Yet consider how many of these conversations reach the levels of being coaching conversations? This might be difficult to answer, but putting time into having coaching conversations can be so helpful in supporting your employees in their role and enhancing their output, commitment, motivation and performance.

So when does a conversation become a coaching conversation? Well, how often do you find yourself in a conversation with an employee where you are telling them what you expect to see, how they should reach the goals, giving them the ideas to hit the targets or solve particular issues? If all of this sounds familiar then changing the approach to use a coaching conversation may provide you with a deeper knowledge of your employees.

Coaching conversations can help discover hidden strengths and talents and elicit ideas, which otherwise may remain dormant or not be realised. How do you do this? Adopting a coaching conversation approach uses a myriad of skills, such as building rapport, listening, questioning, feedback and the use of frameworks and models to structure the conversation. With practice these skills can enable dynamic, engaging and often soul searching and challenging conversations to occur. So instead of you, the manager, doing all the talking and telling, the coaching conversation can start to form with the focus on using skills to elicit the information and realise potential which otherwise may not be tapped into. So it is really a coachee-centred approach, not manager directed.

But where do you start? It takes time to practice all the required skills and techniques to adopt a coaching conversation approach, but the benefits gained can be immense.

The Challenge

Take time out to consider the quality of the conversations you currently have with employees and ask yourself if there is scope to elevate the quality and goals of these to bring greater worth and value. By starting to take some small steps and changes to the conversations you are engaged in, you will be on the first rung of the ladder to taking a more coaching conversation approach.

Four tips for coaching conversations

I've already mentioned GROW as a really useful structure to follow when having a coaching conversation. It stands for GOAL, REALITY, OPTIONS, WAY FORWARD. This is a really important structure to follow during either a single coaching conversation, or one that may take you several sessions.

Here are some key points to help you:

Clear your mind space – When having coaching conversations it is important to ensure the space in your mind is clear and uncluttered. Take a few seconds out prior to entering a conversation to mentally remove the previous task or interaction you have just had. Look to eliminate or park any thoughts regarding the person, how they have performed in the past, how you would like them to perform in the future, any assumptions, perceptions or judgements you may have on them. Your mind should be like a blank piece of paper ready to embrace what you are presented with.

Maximise the moment – Give the person your full focus, without interruptions. Too often conversations are unnecessarily interrupted by technology and other physical or mental demands on us. See the time you set aside as a precious investment.

Listen to them not you – As the manager, how often have you already decided what is the best course of action and you aren't really listening because you know what you want to say and what needs to be done? Consequently you spend more time listening to your own inner voice. Take a step back and listen to what your employees are actually saying, not just to what you want to hear.

Question them, don't tell – Rather than telling people what to do or what you expect to see, start to see how you can incorporate questions to elicit ideas from them. For example: what is happening at the moment? What could you do to change that? What other ideas do you have? How could you make that happen? This is a similar approach to the one I recommended in Management Challenge Number 12: How to Handle Underperformance

These tips are just the start, but please don't underestimate their impact. If you feel you could enhance the quality of conversations you are having and raise them to a coaching conversation level then coaching skills for managers provide a powerful toolset to support this. Start by identifying opportunities when you can employ these tips and experience the power of conversation.

How to run an internal training session

➤ At times you may want to run a short training session for your team. If you haven't got anyone who can help you, here are some of my top secret tips:

➤ Don't decide that 'manager knows best'. Get the group together and ask for their opinions and ideas on the way forward first

➤ Make sure you incorporate these ideas – don't just do your own thing regardless or you'll lose credibility and they won't want to contribute next time

➤ Decide what you want to achieve in the session. Be realistic about the time available and most importantly write the objectives as benefits and results so that you inspire, persuade and increase motivation for the event. Remember the WIIFM principle that drives behaviour: 'What's in it for me' as this will be key to getting involvement and contribution from your team

➤ Structure the session so that you have a mix of training methods. Make it participative and don't drone on out the front and show hundreds of boring bullet-pointed slides

➤ Don't just run the session in the way that would appeal to you. Remember that people learn in different ways so cater for the range of learning styles: activist, pragmatist, theorist and reflector

➤ Provide some fruit, sweets, biscuits or cakes and soft drinks, even if you have to pay for this out of your own pocket. It will be worth it

➤ Take photos of the group work and send them round after to the team and/or upload them into your Learning Management System (LMS) if you have one, for private group view

➢ Do a team-teach at the end to remind everyone of what they have learned

➢ Summarise actions

➢ Make sure something positive changes/happens as a result of the session and celebrate successes

➢ Oh and by the way, you don't always have to be the lead – why not ask a different team member each month to follow your approach and run a short internal session for the team on an area of their expertise?

Here's a useful table which will help you further:

Learning Principles	Implications for course design
The adult is a partner with the facilitator in the learning process	Participants should actively influence the learning approach
Adults are capable of taking responsibility for their own learning	Incorporate self-directed activities in the course design
Adult learners gain through two-way communication	Avoid over-use of lectures and 'talking to', emphasise discussion
Adults learn through reflections on their and others' experience	Use interactive methods such as case studies, role-playing, etc
Adults learn what they perceive to be useful in their life situations	Make the content and materials fit assessed needs
Adults' attention spans are a function of their interest in the experience	Allow plenty of time to 'process' the learning activities

Learning Principles	Implications for course design
Adults are most receptive to instruction that is clearly related to problems they face daily	Include applications planning in each learning activity
Adults learn best when they are being treated with respect	Get them problem solving and affirm the experience of participants
Adults do not typically see themselves as learners	Give participants a rationale for becoming involved and provide opportunities for success
Adults learn better in a climate that is informal and personal	Promote getting acquainted and interpersonal linkages
Adults learners apply learning that they have been influential in planning	Diagnose and prioritise learning needs and preferences during the event as well as before
Adults learn when they feel supported in experimenting with new ideas and skills	Use learning group as 'home bases' for participants
Adults are likely to have somewhat fixed points of view that make them closed to new ways of thinking and behaving	Include interpersonal feedback exercises and opportunities to experiment
Adults learn to react to the differential status of members of the group	Use sub-groups to provide safety and readiness to engage in open interchange
Adults are internally motivated to develop increased effectiveness	Make all learner evaluation self-directed
Adults filter their learning through their value systems	Provide activities that focus on cognitive, and behavioural change

How to facilitate group discussion

As a manager you will often find yourself having to facilitate group discussion, at internal training sessions, breakout groups, team meetings, away days etc.

Here are some of the mistakes that I see managers making so try and avoid these:

- ✗ Coercing
- ✗ Tricking
- ✗ Dictating
- ✗ Giving your own views first
- ✗ Solving the problem yourself
- ✗ Speaking too much
- ✗ Asking closed questions too frequently
- ✗ Asking leading questions
- ✗ Inferring favourites
- ✗ Putting members down

✘ Prejudice, Bias

✘ Assumptions

✘ Too task orientated – ignoring the process

✘ Expecting too much too soon

✘ Ignoring pacing and signalling cues

✘ Poor planning and preparation

✘ Poor listening

✘ Inappropriate body language

Here are some of the skills, tips and tricks to get positive results:

✓ Planning and preparation

✓ Active, perceptive listening and 'attending behaviour'

✓ Appropriate body language

✓ Excellent mastery of question technique

✓ Patience

✓ Observation

✓ Understanding words, ideas and feelings

✓ 'Playback' – summarise and reflect

✓ Be approachable

✓ Make everyone feel important

✓ Take the temperature

✓ Be aware of the synergistic characteristics of the group

✓ Use silence

✓ Avoid the unhelpful behaviours!

Here's a possible framework to help you:

- ➤ Prepare and plan
- ➤ Clarify objectives/outcomes
- ➤ Decide strategy
- ➤ Develop a route map
- ➤ Consider room layout and seating/equipment
- ➤ Welcome members
- ➤ Introductions where necessary
- ➤ Tent cards if appropriate
- ➤ Set the scene
- ➤ Lay out clear ground rules and boundaries if necessary
- ➤ Consider how much information is necessary to enable meaningful contributions
- ➤ "This is your meeting"
- ➤ Low key/low risk early on
- ➤ Careful application of questions
- ➤ Take an early coffee/tea break
- ➤ Manage the 'process' – see previous key skills tips and tricks
- ➤ Summarise, restate any decisions/actions to be taken
- ➤ Thanks

When running meetings, training sessions, and facilitating discussion as well as interviewing, coaching, performance managing, and many other conversations we have as a manager, here's one of my most important tactics. I'm sure it will help you too. It sounds simple but often isn't so you will need to master it. I've mentioned it already several times. It's all about asking questions. In fact, I think it's more than that. It's all about what I call question tactics: so revisit the guidance on open and closed questions and here's my cheat sheet to remind us when and why we ask questions:

Questions Cheat Sheet

- ✓ To seek factual information
- ✓ To provoke discussion
- ✓ To seek personal or expert opinion
- ✓ To provide transition to another phase
- ✓ To direct attention to difficulties/complexities
- ✓ To discover needs
- ✓ To show agreement
- ✓ To show areas of disagreement
- ✓ To discover strengths/weaknesses
- ✓ To discover attitudes
- ✓ To check listening
- ✓ To grab attention
- ✓ To divert
- ✓ To generate interest
- ✓ To discover agendas/motivation
- ✓ To seek reassurance
- ✓ To flatter/boost confidence
- ✓ To demonstrate knowledge/expertise
- ✓ To impart information
- ✓ To allow others to let off steam
- ✓ To demonstrate interest
- ✓ To avoid the answer

✓ To buy time

✓ To stimulate thinking

✓ To consider alternatives

✓ To encourage independence

✓ To help others diagnose their own problems and seek to determine their own solutions

✓ To control

✓ To prevent prolonged discussion of side issues and to avert arguments

✓ To form stepping stones to give direction

Overleaf is a profiling sheet you may like to fill out to check where you think your facilitation style may be now and then mark where you would like it to be. Then plan how you are going to move in a positive direction and seek out opportunities to practice. Chart your progress:

FACILITATOR STYLE PROFILE

Instructions: Think of your manner of facilitating discussion in groups: how you deliver information, set up activities and relate to participants. On each of the twenty-six bi-polar scales below write an "X" to indicate your usual facilitation style. Be honest with yourself. Then go back and circle those adjectives that describe how you would like to improve. This will help you develop an agenda for your professional development as a group facilitator.

Withholds support	1.	Gives support
Not participating	2.	Participating
Talking at	3.	Talking with
Impractical	4.	Practical
Not open about self	5.	Open about self
Unfriendly	6.	Friendly
Disorganised	7.	Organised
Sober	8.	Humorous
Inflexible	9.	Flexible
Insensitive to others' needs	10.	Sensitive to others' needs
Does not relate to	11.	Makes things happen
Unclear	12.	Clear
Cold	13.	Warm
Aloof	14.	Approachable
Limited in resource	15.	Resourceful
Slow	16.	Quick
Unimaginative	17.	Creative

Uses few techniques	18.	Uses many techniques
Avoids confrontation	19.	Confronts
Relationship oriented	20.	Results oriented
Imposing	21.	Allowing
Tense	22.	Relaxed
Formal	23.	Informal
Makes things complicated	24.	Makes things simple
Serious	25.	Playful
Playing safe	26.	Taking risks

Alison facilitating table-work at one of her management events

Informal learning: ideas and opportunities

To ensure your own success as a manager you'll also be wanting to make the most of informal learning opportunities in your organisation, for yourself and your team. And that goes further than running internal training sessions and meetings.

In fact there's loads you can do to create a culture that helps people learn, develop and improve informally, every day.

Here are some ideas to maximise informal learning opportunities to build your team development that often cost little or nothing to implement yet bring a fantastic return:

- Adopt a mentoring and coaching culture
- Day-to-Day interactions and reflection
- Observational feedback
- Formal and informal discussions
- Set up communities of practice
- Delegation
- Encourage operating in stretch zones
- Staff blogs
- Guided projects
- Interactive training theatre
- Air and Shares
- 'Know how' bulletins
- Table top sessions
- Brown Bag lunches
- Hot Button issues
- Cheat sheets

- ➢ Sneak Peaks

- ➢ Sharing success stories

- ➢ Temporary projects: job-swapping, ad-hoc projects, matrix team membership

- ➢ If budgets are really tight, a guided project can give someone exposure to new knowledge. It can develop new skills and even give someone an opportunity to experience cross-boundary working.

- ➢ Choose the right person and a real-life project. Then guide them through it. You'd normally relinquish control and input the more the person becomes familiar with the work involved.

Here are some of my most favourite informal learning tools:

➢ Reflective journals

Keep one of these yourself and encourage all your staff to have one too. It's just a little book you keep with you and in which you jot down reflections, useful learnings and observations from your day to day work, as well as courses, so that you can store this up and revisit. It's such a simple idea. I've used it for years and have kept a whole series of them in my filing cabinet. I regularly check them and always find something new to implement. People tell me they love this inexpensive and easy tool to encourage responsibility for one's own learning and development, to implement and review ideas and to promote a continuous learning culture. And it's so cost-effective!

➢ Set up a 'Lunch with...'

Set up a session every so often to get one team networking with another. You could even do the same with your manager- people could put their names down for a restricted numbers lunch.

They then get a chance to meet and chat over with senior people ideas and issues in the business. This works well if you are looking to change the culture of your business, to break down silos and also enable senior people to be more accessible.

➤ Action Learning Sets

Apparently once described as a 'simple, elegant process – better experienced than explained', action learning is a well-respected method for management learning and development. So, put simply, an action learning set comprises a group of managers, normally between 4 and 7 works best. The set then meets regularly to support one another in their learning so that they can discuss and then progress work issues, problems and challenges. It gives members of the set the opportunity to learn from each other and engage in a shared learning. It also enables you to deal with the kind of management problems which cannot be easily resolved through lectures or seminars and helps to build up strong networks and relationships.

I've been using action learning sets to strengthen management development programmes for more than 20 years and they always add such value. There are some particular skills and techniques needed, so you will need to have trained facilitators or go on a course yourself.

Invite more junior or inexperienced members of your team to take part in more senior meetings. Brief everyone clearly beforehand. It will give them and the existing group a fresh perspective.

➤ Find and use your internal champions.

You know the ones I'm talking about: those who embrace new ideas, look for the positives, generally see change as a good thing and are passionate about their own learning. Seek out these people; offer them a voluntary role to champion changes you want to bring about.

These people are great at rallying others behind them and can be instrumental in helping to introduce and embed new ways of working and attitudinal and behavioural changes.

So there's much you can drive yourself.

These are just a few ideas on how you can make informal learning a way of life at work. Continual and informal learning is becoming a 'must have' for any organisation valuing its people.

Top 15 takeaways to accelerate your success when developing your team...and yourself

- ✓ Recognise the development of your staff as a continual top priority
- ✓ Devise a range of blended learning opportunities within the workplace
- ✓ Practise your coaching skills and act as a coach to your staff
- ✓ Run internal training sessions for your team
- ✓ Get them to take responsibility and remember WIIFM
- ✓ Familiarise yourself with the key principles of adult learning
- ✓ Practise facilitating group discussions using my guidelines
- ✓ Use the questions cheat sheet to increase your understanding of the power of questions and when and how to use them. Work on refining your strategy with questions
- ✓ Review your facilitator profile regularly
- ✓ Select at least 4 informal learning opportunities from the list and put into action over the next month
- ✓ Keep a reflective journal and encourage your staff to have one too

✓ Get an action learning set going for your team or one for yourself – or both!

✓ Find and use your internal champions

✓ Set up 'Lunch with...'

✓ **Continually use this book to accelerate your success as a manager!**

MANAGEMENT CHALLENGE NUMBER 15: HOW TO MANAGE INDIVIDUAL CONTRIBUTORS

Secrets to support professionals who don't want to climb the management ladder

What do you call that professional you manage who doesn't have line management responsibilities, who works as an individual but who contributes significantly to the goals and mission of your team and therefore the organisation?

There is a new phrase that is being used to describe the role of the senior professional who works without people management responsibilities. This is the 'Individual Contributor'.

You may well have one of these in your team. They are really skilled operationally or professionally. In fact they are probably indispensable to you. The challenge for you as their manager is probably going to be to work out how to harness the value that such 'Individual Contributors' can make. Just because they don't want to move into management roles does not mean you can leave them to stagnate. You need to look at their development path and opportunities very carefully or you may risk losing them.

One of the questions that HR departments struggle with is whether their development programmes are missing out support for some of these key individuals? After all, because 'Individual Contributors' often have job titles that do not contain the title 'Manager' or 'Director' they may be overlooked when it comes to investment in developing these important team members within the organisation and as such a pool of people with potential and influence is at risk of being overlooked, side-lined and demotivated.

The phenomenon of influence shows us that it is not always linked to a person's position in an organisational hierarchy.

I think that it is fair to say that a person's position does not always define their contribution, nor does it give an indication of the person's true influence on others. We have all found some individuals with big titles and yet in reality they are not always influential. We can sometimes find those who despite their titles do not make major contributions. The opposite is also true: there are some people without a managerial title who wield a significant amount of influence and make fantastic contributions, regardless of their title or role.

So contribution may not be simply defined by role or title. I've found many such individuals who have preferred or chosen not to pursue management careers, but instead have followed their interest in a professional skills set. These people are the highly professional individual contributors. However, they exist across many organisations: sometimes it is the statistician in a think tank, the sector specialist in an insurance underwriting function, the software engineer in a high tech company, the key sales person in a sales team.

These 'individual contributors' might well need encouragement in your team. Given their level of contribution it would make sense to ensure that they feel highly valued. Put a retention strategy together to keep them and think about how you can go about harness their informal but effective influence.

You could be missing out on the opportunity to retain these key people, to help them be even more influential and to prepare a portion of them for key positions in the organisation. Losing them can be a huge and expensive blow to your business, but often they fail to show up on anyone's radar screen. So ensure they do on yours.

Top 6 takeaways to accelerate your success when developing individual contributors in your team

- ✓ Identify your individual contributors and encourage them to increase their sphere of influence for the good of the team

- ✓ Ensure in your 1:1s you have discussions with individual contributors to map out opportunities for development

- ✓ Make them feel valued but remember equity theory – don't give preferential treatment

- ✓ Make it clear it's fine not to want to go into management and up that proverbial ladder

- ✓ Encourage them to think laterally about how they can expand their experience

- ✓ Secondments, job rotation, job enrichment and mentoring can work really well as development tools as well as the other informal learning opportunities suggested in Management Challenge 14

Alison Miles-Jenkins

MANAGEMENT CHALLENGE NUMBER 16: HOW TO GET YOUR TEAM CUSTOMER/CLIENT FOCUSSED

The secrets to leading a great customer experience team culture

For more than two decades I've been a champion of good customer experience. My passion for quality, care in our interactions with others and a determination to succeed drives everything in my life. It is pivotal to running my business, my relationship with my team, my clients, my delegates, my coachees, contacts, and suppliers. It seeps into my personal life, and infects, positively, I hope, my family, my kids and my friends.

So you can imagine how disappointed I constantly feel as a customer, as I'm sure you do too, when I experience a shocking lack of customer care. From the waiters of the newly opened restaurant not far from here, to the bored receptionist, the inept call centre agent, the disinterested 'not my job' council officer, to the hotel staff who are taught to say 'Good morning' but not how to say sorry when something goes wrong. Perhaps I am not typically British – I will give feedback, and I will complain. My kids – not yet worn down enough as customers – whisper "Mum, don't start!"

For more than 25 years I have been working with client

organisations to help them stand out, to differentiate their services, by paying more attention to the personal side of service, and not just the material side - an obsession with their products, services and shareholder value.

So I understand only too well that to align a collection of individuals and to motivate them all to want to deliver a good customer experience is a huge challenge, but it is not impossible. Most of the time though as a customer I am disappointed and disillusioned, and find myself comparing customer experience here unfavourably with our European, American and other counterparts.

Is it not strange that, given the ongoing challenging environment in which we all work these days, those responsible for strategy and performance in organisations rarely have customer experience on their agendas? Don't they feel the need not just for satisfied customers, but for loyal ones, who will champion and advocate for them? Don't they understand the power of turning round complainants and the subsequent increase in their repurchase intention?

What I have discovered time and again over the years is that any business which wants to get its customer experience right has to put its employees first. And this means you being a great manager (and following the advice in this book!).

I've identified that staff with positive attitudes towards their manager are able to share that positivity with customers. I've also learnt that these employees are those with the 'magic sauce'. By this I mean they are willing and able to go that extra mile to give great service and resolve let downs and complaints. That extra mile is often referred to in HR circles as that 'discretionary extra effort'.

Customers are happy when they deal with highly trained and skilled staff who are content and competent in their role. They respond well to staff with a 'can do attitude', or 'positive mental attitude', searching for solutions and resolutions rather than a focus on what can't be done. This empowerment shows in their body language, verbal behaviour and ability to build rather than destroy a relationship with the customer. But where does that come from? It comes from a focus on both employee engagement (by you being a great manager) and customer experience.

How might we define an 'engaged' member of staff? Let's consider the following wish list:

An employee who:

- Demonstrates consistently going that extra mile with customers. They give that 'discretionary' effort

- Clearly and consistently shows understanding of their work goals

- 'Gets it' from a business perspective and truly buys into the team and business goals

- Benefits from a productive two way relationship with their manager

- Is motivated and satisfied by their work role and responsibilities

- Works productively and demonstrates consistent high performance

Whilst great recruitment and selection strategies can go a long way to getting employees with the right attitude and potential on board in the first place as I demonstrated in Management Challenge Number 2, management style, organisational culture, communication barriers and lack of training and coaching can easily demotivate. Worse still, these can lead to a high churn rate.

Add to this the social element of customer experience and the real need for advocacy and positive word of mouth from delighted customers, we should also consider employee/brand ambassadorship.

So as a manager here are some of the practical things you need to do with your team:

- Encourage them to think of the customer as someone they need, not who needs them

- Customer Experience– build it into your team strategically and operationally

- Build customer experience responsibility into every job description from the top down. Build customer experience skills and attitudes into every person specification from the top down.

- Select the right people – think about whether you are building customer experience, attitudes and skills **appropriately** into your person specifications – for **all** posts. How are you testing this?

- Transform your team culture into one which truly values and nurtures each member

- Walk the talk. As a manager role model the right behaviours and attitudes with customers, as this will infect the staff

- Don't treat your staff as though they don't count. Remember, we humans pass on treatment.

- Empower your staff. Inspire and motivate them. Learn from them.

- Ensure your procedures and policies are there to help the customers and staff, not hinder them. They shouldn't be there just for organisational comfort

- How much front-line ownership is there? Staff must be able and willing, without fear of recrimination, to respond effectively to customer needs

- Train, support, praise, reinforce, monitor and feed back

- Job satisfaction leads to excellent customer experience which leads to job satisfaction

- Build customer experience performance into every review/appraisal from the top down

- Ensure that customer experience is on the agenda of team meetings every time. I don't just mean complaints and systems issues. I mean have a proactive item, encouraging honest discussion and a conscious and continual search for development and improvement opportunities and ideas

- Testing Testing Testing! Mystery shop your own services at least twice a year and act on the results. Whatever you do, do not make the mistake of putting your most junior, least experienced, lowest paid members of staff as the first point of contact for your customers or clients. Why on earth do managers do that?

Finally, please remember – keep working at it – one run round the block won't make you fit – regular exercise will! It's a constantly moving horizon – so continually develop, revisit, reinvent and improve. For further advice on this why not check out our ECI© model at

www.newmanagersecrets.com/resources

Top 12 takeaways to accelerate your team's success with customer experience

- ✓ Develop employees to have 'magic sauce' - willing and able to go that extra mile
- ✓ Focus on both employee engagement (by you being a great manager) and customer experience.
- ✓ Encourage your team to think of the customer as someone they need, not who needs them
- ✓ Customer Experience– build it into your team strategically and operationally
- ✓ Select the right people – think about whether you are building customer experience attitudes and skills **appropriately** into your person specifications
- ✓ Walk the talk. As a manager role model the right behaviours and attitudes with customers
- ✓ Don't treat your staff as though they don't count. Remember, we humans pass on treatment.
- ✓ Train, support, praise, reinforce, monitor and feed back
- ✓ Build customer experience performance into every review/appraisal from the top down
- ✓ Ensure that customer experience is on the agenda of team meetings every time
- ✓ Mystery shop your own services at least twice a year and act on the results
- ✓ Keep working at it – one run round the block won't make you fit – regular exercise will! It's a constantly moving horizon – so continually develop

Action Point for Immediate Implementation!

Put customer experience on the next team meeting agenda and lead the way.

Commit to a date now:

Judging the customer service training awards 2013

MANAGEMENT CHALLENGE NUMBER 17: HOW TO HANDLE COMPLAINTS

The secrets to resolving let downs and customer complaints

As a manager you'll get complaints from time to time – from staff, colleagues, your boss, your customers/clients etc.

Complaints handling can sometimes be seen as a "mystic art". Some people think that only those who are experts at it can be expected to succeed and most of those can only be found in specialist areas such as regulators or complaints services.

Fortunately, for you and for me, this is a myth. Handling and resolving complaints well is actually fairly simple, because in essence it is a process. Applying a process is enhanced by simply learning some key skills.

You can learn how to become much better in handling tricky interactions so that complaints are reduced in number or even don't happen at all. This will give you a competitive edge, build your reputation, and allow you to justify higher prices for your products and services with external customers.

Here's an overview of the key strategies for successful complaints resolution:

1. **Awareness** – make sure all your team know what a complaint is, how to recognise it and how to respond. This means you have to define and share what a complaint actually means to you.

2. **Acknowledge** – get the person on side quickly; show you are taking the complaint seriously. Acknowledge the issue and the emotions expressed behind the complaint. From experience we rarely do this naturally but have to be trained.

3. **Respond** – don't be defensive, be positive. You can resolve this and usually achieve a win/win outcome for you and the other person. You will need to use some of the key interpersonal and communication skills we've already covered under other Management Challenges to excel at this.

4. **Follow through** – keep your promises and check to be sure that the other person regards the resolution you've agreed with them as the end to the complaint.

5. **Learn** – if the complaint can be avoided next time by a change in procedure, communication or advice don't lose that lesson.

6. **Mindset Change** – this can be transformational. Get your staff to think of handling resolutions rather than complaints. Resolution is a wonderful, positive word and avoids the negative connotations and emotions that the word 'complaint' can bring with it.

In every complaint whether it is a really complex issue or a wrangle over price or service, considering these six elements will give you the edge to resolving that complaint.

Here's more detail and guidance to help you handle complaints with external customers, clients, patients etc. Please note that if you work in a regulated environment there will be other procedures and considerations that you have to take into account.

1. Awareness of complaints

One of the biggest challenges to excellent complaints responsiveness is getting the team to be fully aware of what a complaint is, and what a complaint is not. Your business will have procedures for dealing with a complaint and they should be up to date and well understood by all. If your complaints handling procedures are gathering dust then it is time to blow the covering off and review them. Your team need to understand how complaints resolution will work in your business so they need to read and understand these procedures. If you find that your procedures are old and out-dated we can help improve them and support you with embedding these procedures so the staff are at ease with them and can easily call upon them if they need to.

Many complaints escalate because they are not recognised when they first occur. Sometimes dismissed as minor grumbles, what first appear as minor complaints can sour a relationship over time. Minor grumbles can build up and the issue that appears to cause the complaint may not be the root cause but simply the final straw.

So your team need to be on the look-out for any expression of dissatisfaction, whether justified in your view or not, so that can it be dealt with as a complaint. After all that is the definition of a complaint given by the British Standards Institute.

Awareness of complaints will also drive a real desire in the team to have excellent and clear communication with your customers. Complaints about price, service and durability can be minimised by managing expectations at the outset. Making sure your team have excellent communication skills and that your communications are joined up across the team are essential strategies.

Real awareness is the starting point for great complaints resolution.

2. Acknowledging complaints

Having made sure that you are on top of the complaints awareness issues, you will want to think about how you acknowledge complaints when they are received.

Complaints arise when people don't get the service they expect. It's vital to give customers who make a complaint a helpful response. The reasoning behind this is that by demonstrating to the customer that you are taking their complaint seriously and want to resolve it you can really make all the difference. It's really, really important to acknowledge the other person's point of view. It is often inappropriate to try and persuade a customer to do what you want; instead it is better to understand what they want, and then try to help them achieve it.

Acknowledging the complaint, explaining what you are going to do to resolve it and telling the complainant when to expect resolution will show you are serious about it. If the matter is complex it may take some time to investigate, particularly if you have to deal with third parties etc. If that happens make sure the customer knows that they haven't been forgotten; don't keep them in the dark. Keep them informed. The key word is 'resolution'; so keep thinking you are handling a resolution, not a complaint. It's all about a mind-set change to help you achieve better results.

When first acknowledging a complaint a genuine apology can establish empathy. Remember an apology is not the same as an admission of guilt or liability.

3. How to respond

Speed is often of the essence when resolving complaints - the longer it takes the more difficult it becomes.

A complaint made in person if not dealt with quickly can be the subject of a written/email complaint. Then chaser letters follow, more letters to other authorities follow that. All of this activity is usually because the complaint is not being dealt with quickly enough.

The reason why customers can and do behave in this way is that it feels to them like they are not being taken seriously if their complaint takes a long time to be dealt with. Worst of all is when you are investigating and working on a complaint but the customer doesn't know and simply assumes you are ignoring them. So please don't fall into that particular trap.

So you need to move quickly if a complaint is received. I have experienced a Director in one of our client organisations receiving a complaint, putting it in his briefcase to deal with, then going off on holiday and forgetting about it until his return. He was filled with great intentions but lost two weeks with nothing happening other than the customer was becoming even more annoyed. Make sure your processes can deal with the complaint, even when you are not there. Colleagues can deal with it, gather information, and keep in touch with the customer.

A big issue here is to try to avoid becoming defensive. It may feel like an assault on your professionalism or an attack on you personally. In reality a customer has not received what they expected in some way and that needs dealing with professionally. Differing expectations between your people and the customer on an issue are often the root cause. So recognising that this might be more about communication than simply a defect in the product or service is half the battle.

If you haven't asked the customer what would resolve the complaint when you first received it make sure you do before offering a solution. Often long rambling complaints cover every minor issue as a way of raising the importance of the complaint to make you take notice. Solving one of these might simply be the key. You won't know unless you ask.

If the complaint is justified offer a fair solution, which might involve action to put things right if you have made a mistake.

When offering a solution to a customer keep in mind these key points:

They want an explanation of the events leading to their complaint.

They want an apology.

They want an assurance that the same mistakes will not be made in the future.

4. Follow through on complaints

It's crucial that having solved the complaint with a resolution don't risk having it restart by not doing what you said you will do. Keep your promises and make a courtesy call to the customer to make sure that the matter is resolved. If it isn't, keeping your head down will make matters worse. It will start all over again so it makes sense to deal with it proactively now.

By saying how sorry you are that something has gone wrong can be all that is needed to turn a complainant into an advocate.

5. Learn from complaints

Having dealt with the complaint take a chance to review what went wrong. Borrow from the project management discipline and undertake a 'lessons learned' review. Get your team to consider the complaint, what caused it, how it was handled and learn from that to improve your customer experience. That way, the effort put into resolving that complaint will be an investment in your business and professional reputation rather than simply an overhead.

Review your complaints procedure. Procedures often read well but it is not until they are used that any flaws or omissions become apparent. Polishing the procedure up and making sure the team are familiar with it will be a good investment.

6. Mindset Change

Remember! This can be transformational. Get your staff to think of handling resolutions rather than complaints. Resolution is a wonderful, positive word isn't it and it avoids the negative connotations and emotions that the word 'complaint' can bring with it. We've had such good feedback on this one point alone on our training courses. It really does make a difference.

So there we have the basics to successful complaints handling: Six essential strategies to ensure your complaints resolution is successful. You can start today in your business making sure that your complaints handling is the best it can be, using my strategies to help you.

These fundamentals if you apply them rigorously will make a huge difference to your complaints handling.

Imagine what would happen to your business if you started to make these changes in the way you deal with complaints... how will that affect your team performance? Your profits would increase and your costs would reduce.

Always remember that many customers give up complaining at the first hurdle, or decide it is not worth bothering with. The problem goes away because so does the customer. However, you can guarantee they'll tell around ten, perhaps twenty other people about your organisation and what they think of you! The result? Loss of business and reputational risk.

Top 6 takeaways to accelerate your success with complaints handling

✓ **Awareness** – make sure all your team know what a complaint is, how to recognise it and how to respond

✓ **Acknowledge** – get the person on-side quickly; show you are taking the complaint seriously. Acknowledge the issue and the emotions expressed behind the complaint.

✓ **Respond** – don't be defensive, be positive. You can resolve this and usually achieve a win/win outcome for you and the other person.

✓ **Follow through** – keep your promises

✓ **Learn** – if the complaint can be avoided next time by a change in procedure, communication or advice don't lose that lesson.

✓ **Mind-set Change** – this can be transformational. Get your staff to think of handling resolutions rather than complaints.

Action Point for Immediate Implementation!

Check out your complaints procedures. Then run a mini training session for your team on the procedures and the top 6 takeaways above. You can also incorporate the guidance from Management Challenge Number 14: How To Develop Your Team, and focus on the tips for running an internal training session and facilitating group discussion.

MANAGEMENT CHALLENGE NUMBER 18: HOW TO DEVELOP A WINNING MIND-SET

The secrets to thinking you can, rather than thinking you can't

Sir Bob Geldof and Alison Miles-Jenkins 23 July 2010 London

As a manager you are going to need a winning mind-set. Your team will need a winning mind-set. If you are aspiring to be a manager, you'll need a winning mind-set.

I've already shared with you that achievement means a lot to me personally and so I was really inspired when I met Sir Bob Geldof some years ago. He is surely one of the greatest contemporary achievers. Remember what he accomplished with Band Aid and Live Aid when £100 million was raised for African famine relief? Recall his challenging of Margaret Thatcher, leading to a major re-evaluation of British government policy towards famine relief and all his subsequent achievements. His accolades go on and on.

Musical and political history was made by this man. Listening to him I was so inspired to learn about his journey through life, the way he opened up his mind to possibilities that others would not have been able to see, and his staggering ability to challenge and to influence.

So when we are at work, how much do we really open our minds to the infinite possibilities that are out there, just waiting to be identified and optimised? We can't change where we started from but we can certainly change where we end up. How do we open our minds?

I've listed below some simple but provocative ideas and thoughts that may help you because they have helped me along the way:

1. Change your view of failure

Successful people fail more often. This is partly due to the way they view trial and error. If they try something and it doesn't work, they look at the end result they have achieved as purely that. A result. Not a failure. They don't see failure. They see purely the results, the opportunity to move on, and try something else. So when learning how to manage people, accept it won't always go as you planned, particularly if you are trying a new approach. So....

Reframe failure as a natural result of learning

2. Check your attitudes

A winning attitude can achieve anything – believe this and help your team to believe this too.

3. Access an amazing formula

Combine attitude and skill and you will find you have an amazing formula. Create a culture of positive thinking and belief and ensure everyone has the right tools to do the job. You should see the skill levels rising.

4. A weekly obligation

Ask yourself and your team every week "What have you done to improve the business this week?"

5. Exercise your brain

Our brain is a staggering piece of kit. Ensure you know how to access the bits you don't habitually use. Mind mapping courses, and advanced creative thinking and learning techniques can really help with this.

6. Get a fresh pair of eyes

Do you look at your business and your team as though it is your first day? If not, do so and think what you would change. Start that plan today.

7. Adopt an attitude of gratitude

Adopt an attitude of gratitude – at the end of each day/week write a list of the positive things (however small) you have experienced during that time. This encourages you to be grateful for the small things that you may not usually notice.

8. Talk to strangers

Talk to strangers! The more people you meet the more opportunities you are creating for yourself. If you are looking to change jobs or to meet a new partner you cannot expect it to happen if you are sitting on the sofa watching TV. You have to make the effort – strike up conversations on the bus, train, in the supermarket checkout. You will be surprised at what happens.

9. Talk to yourself

Talk to yourself! Your brain responds to the 'inner voice' you use to talk to yourself. If your inner voice is constantly critical or moaning then your behaviour will be negative. A positive attitude starts with positive thoughts.

10. Develop new interests

Develop new interests – research has shown that people with hobbies are less stressed and happier than those without. Instead of saying "I wish I could dance/cook/sing" make a decision to learn!

11. Adopt positive body language

It is almost impossible to feel positive when sitting slumped at your desk, head in hands. Changing your body language to an alert upright posture will help change your mind-set.

12. Take exercise

Take exercise. It produces 'feel good' chemicals which your body and brain respond to positively. You might even make new friends this way.

13. Say 'Yes' more often

Say 'yes' more often instead of automatically rejecting opportunities that come your way. Say 'yes' to something different. It might be trying a new restaurant, working on a new project, making a presentation or just volunteering for something that nobody else wants to do. We usually regret the opportunities that we didn't take in life rather than those we did take.

14. Give feedback

Give people feedback. If you admire the way your boss managed a particular project tell them – don't just tell everyone else. If you are appreciative of the work a colleague has done for you, tell them. Likewise it is important to let people know when you are not so happy with things so that they have the chance to put them right.

15. Surround yourself with positive people

There are certain people who boost your energy and others who drain it away. Make a decision to be in the positive crowd, limit spending time with 'energy drainers' who just depress and exhaust you. It is generally recognised that our attitude towards a situation has a direct bearing on the outcome. Every day we demonstrate both positive and negative behaviours towards people which affect how they in turn feel about us. This can be the start of a vicious circle (negative) or a vital cycle (positive).

Any manager knows that it can take considerable time to build up and nurture the morale of a team, yet negativity can take hold in just a few minutes. This can have a detrimental effect on motivation and productivity.

16. Set goals

Set goals and reward yourself when you have achieved them. If the goals appear too daunting and far-off break them down into bite-size chunks to make them more achievable.

17. Get an accountability partner

This is someone who you can check in with, share your goal with and report progress. You are more likely to be successful with whatever you want to achieve in life, at work and at play, if you get yourself an accountability partner.

By having the right mind-set, recruiting the right person for the job, motivating them, showing good leadership, delegating, managing your own time and their performance, getting the team working well together and knowing what to do when things go wrong, you will be significantly reducing the frustrations that come with being a people manager.

Top 10 takeaways to accelerate your success with a winning mind-set

- ✓ Try something new or different. If it works - great. If it doesn't, think of it as a result. Try again

- ✓ Believe in yourself – a winning attitude can achieve anything

- ✓ Upskill yourself and add your newfound abilities to your mind-set. That's powerful stuff

- ✓ Look at your business weekly and ask what you have done to improve it

- ✓ Keep increasing your connections and have a network, as well as an accountability partner

- ✓ Exercise your brain and your body for maximum results

- ✓ Use positive body language to project an aura of confidence

- ✓ Analyse your self-talk and reject the negative dialogue

- ✓ Surround yourself with people who are where you want to be

- ✓ Don't just think about what you want to achieve. Go out and do it.

What are you going to do right now to implement changes to your mind-set and get you to that winning post?

Alison with the amazing, inspirational Sean Stephenson

Alison with Marcus Lemonis, 'The Profit'
People. Process. Product.

Write your plan below with actions and deadlines, and a column to fill in once you've implemented with your successes, results and further implementation plans.

MANAGEMENT CHALLENGE NUMBER 19: HOW TO START CLIMBING THE MANAGEMENT LADDER

The secrets to a CV that gets you in the interview chair

If you are thinking of applying for your first management position, or you are considering the next step up then this is going to be really helpful for you.

The sad truth about CVs is here

The sad truth is that most CVs only get a brief look through when we apply for a job. Seems unfair, doesn't it, when we've spent hours putting one together, maybe writing and rewriting it, tweaking and polishing it because we so want that next job.

Your CV has to immediately hit all the right buttons for the busy team members who have been tasked with short-listing applicants for interview. So, how do you make your CV stand out and ensure that it goes to the top of the pile and gets you that coveted place in the interviewee's chair?

Here are 7 of my top tips to help you produce a CV that catches the eye and makes you stick in the recruiter's mind.

Think of your CV as your personal representative.

If you were sending someone to represent you you'd want them to do a great job wouldn't you? Look at your CV with as much scrutiny. It's got to look good. Visual appeal is very important for creating a fantastic first impression. These days we live in a very visual society and there is a widely held view "that if it doesn't look good, it can't be good". First impressions are formed unbelievably quickly. So make sure it's a great representative of you. Clearly written, concise, with lots of white space, unfolded, uncreased and good quality paper and ink are vital ingredients. Don't use lots of different fonts, colours, designs or images. These tend to make it look too busy, fussy or simply that you are trying too hard. The same rules apply if you are making online applications rather than through hard copy CVs.

An insider's view

Guess what? Make the short-lister's life easier. I know, from training literally thousands of people over the years in how to recruit and select staff, that most people do not enjoy having to recruit a new member of staff – unless they have chosen to be a recruitment specialist and that's certainly not most managers! The whole process takes time, there's lots of legalities and skills involved and some people even find it quite nerve-wracking. It's quite a risk when you think about it, isn't it, taking on a new team member? So you will 'score points' if you make it easy for the recruiting managers to do their job. Because of the way the economy is going, they may at the moment be swamped with applications for some positions. So get on their side straight away by:

> Keeping your CV to a maximum of 2 sides of A4

> Make sure you have tailored your CV to the role and not used a generic one

> ➤ Write it in benefits-driven language – that means tell them what you can do for them and the value-add they would get from short-listing you

> ➤ Use a good, easy to follow structure and layout

> ➤ Make sure an electronic CV looks as good as a hard copy

Avoid Common Mistakes

One of the most common mistakes I see all the time with CVs is a focus on listing tasks, not achievements. Again, focus on achievements and benefits that you will bring, not a boring list of tasks.

Check nothing is missing

Leave nothing unaccounted for. If the dates don't add up or there is an obvious break in your employment timeline, account for this. Otherwise the short-lister will make their own assumptions, and these may be well off mark!

This one will put your CV in the bin!

Nothing is more guaranteed to consign your efforts to the bin than spelling mistakes and typing errors. Always proof-read from a hard copy and get someone else to double check it too.

Speak the same language!

To show that you are on the right wavelength and build rapport through your CV, make sure you weave in the right words – words which that organisation specifically uses. To do this re-read the job advert, the job description and the person specification if you have these and incorporate in your CV the same words they are using when they describe what they are seeking.

Use Power words

Every word has to count in your CV so positive, power words convey the right messages that your short-listers will connect with. Examples to get you started are: 'achieved', 'demonstrated', 'exceeded', 'won', 'developed', 'effectively' and 'unique'. Oh, and put down quantifiable figures like targets you reached or exceeded, with examples.

So, follow the tips above to power-boost your CV. That way you'll increase your chances of getting that invitation to interview.

How to use this insider information when you are the candidate

Now of course all the tips, tricks, skills and techniques I shared with you in Management Challenge Number 2: How to recruit and select the best person for the job, will be like a magic wand to you when it comes to applying for your first or next management position. It's always good isn't it to have insider information. I can guarantee the other candidates won't have the same level of knowledge on all of this as you will have (providing you've read this book and they haven't of course!).

Remember this: to protect your livelihood nothing can be more important than knowing how to succeed at interviews. So read on:

20 top tips to succeed at interviews

At interview to ensure you stand out but still fit in remember the following:

1. Never sit in reception whilst waiting. Remain standing – it commands more attention. Sitting down means you lose your height advantage, inhibits your breathing and could make you look like a sales rep!

2. Read some of the articles in reception – newsletters etc while you are waiting and look for opportunities to weave the information into your answers at the interview.

3. The meet and greet is vital. Always offer a firm handshake, smile and create a relaxed, confident first impression.

4. Ensure you have some 'pleasantries' up your sleeve so you can chat on the way to the interview room.

5. Put yourself in the interviewers' shoes. From the moment you are met in reception, you need to be building a relationship. Look at yourself from your interviewers' perspectives. What do they need? What are they looking for? How can you match this?

6. In the interview don't hold your portfolio, bag or briefcase. Put this down by your chair.

7. Ensure you are very familiar with what you have put on your application for this particular job. This is crucial if you are applying for several jobs as it is likely that you will have 'tweaked' your information to suit.

8. If it's a panel interview, you must persuade all the members, not just the one who has asked the question. So make sure you make eye contact with all interviewers.

9. Address panel members by name but don't overuse this.

10. Always have some great questions to ask. For example, 'What is the most pressing problem you would like me to solve?' 'Please

tell me more about the culture of your organisation'.

11. Many interviewers who are well trained will choose to use behavioural type questions. These are open questions, and they will often be followed by further supplementary 'probing' questions. They will use these as they know this makes it very hard for candidates to waffle, evade and lie.

Examples of such lines of questioning include:

"Tell me about a situation recently when you had to handle an under-performing member of your team."

"Why did you choose that particular approach?"

"How effective was it?"

"What did you learn from this?"

"What would you do differently next time?"

"Why?"

So make sure in your preparation you identify specific examples of all the criteria that the employer is seeking. Test yourself with questions and answers such as these.

12. Keep your body language open and relaxed. Make sure you maintain this even when you are finding a question difficult.

13. If you are unsure of the question, or need to buy yourself thinking it over time, ask for clarification.

14. Never ask if you have answered the question.

15. Try and keep some of your sentences under 20 words.

16. Watch your pace – if you gabble you will look nervous. If you gabble and use long sentences you will really be in trouble – you will run out of breath. Your vocal quality will be impaired. Your brainpower will be inhibited. You may lose your train of thought and your interviewers will get bored! They will also forget the relevant points you did make!

17.   Use pause, pace and intonation to add impact to what you say and how you say it.

18.   Don't give dated examples – generally the pace of change is such these days that people are only really interested in what you have achieved during the last two or three years.

19.   Talk benefits of what you have achieved rather than tasks you carry out.

20. Lastly, be on your guard at reception, the 'meet the team' event or the 'tour of the office'.   You are probably still being interviewed.

Top 2 takeaways to accelerate your success with your CV and interviews

✓ Re-read this entire challenge again and update your CV

✓ Re-read this entire challenge again and keep all 20 interview tips up your sleeve for when you next need them.

MANAGEMENT CHALLENGE NUMBER 20: HOW TO GET TO THE ROOM AT THE TOP

The secrets to what you must do now if you want to go all the way

I thought the top is a very good place to finish because a small percentage of you will have your eye on the coveted room at the top. The role of the CEO. If not now, then sometime later perhaps.

You'll need to learn loads that can't possibly go into this book but here's some tips and takeaways to get you thinking:

- ✓ Getting ahead is 10% brains and 90% determination

- ✓ Your attitude will mark you out so decide now you will be the can do, will do person who delivers

- ✓ Most of your competitors will be lazy, lack focus and trivial so be the opposite

- ✓ Sign up for eye catching projects, but take care to make sure that these projects are the ones that the most senior managers support

- ✓ Keep your eye on the strategic tasks: make sure you do exceedingly well the things that are important to your boss, their boss and key influencers. Doing a great job which is noticed only by your colleagues makes you popular perhaps but gets you nowhere.

- ✓ Never moan about colleagues; you don't know who knows who

- ✓ On social occasions take part, but never over indulge. Always be professional – even when out after work with colleagues have the attitude that you are still at work.

- ✓ If you aim for the moon, you will hit the sky. Don't aim too low, have ambitious goals.

- ✓ Identify who in the management team is going places and make yourself indispensable to them, so as they go up the ladder so do you. However, don't put all your eggs in one basket.

- ✓ Don't stay too long in a role, always be looking for that next move up.

- ✓ Know the figures: understand the financials and other data so you can quote key statistics when you need to impress.

- ✓ Make sure your qualifications match your goals. Get an MBA for example, make sure it is from a 'top 10' business school.

- ✓ Be tough on performance; you cannot afford to let poor performance in your team reflect on you. Manage firmly and fairly, in accordance with this book and your procedures.

- ✓ Take care on social media as your social life is something that should be kept private. A good test is to ask yourself: "Would this embarrass me or my employer if I were reading this post in the Daily Mail."

- ✓ Start creating your Dream 100 network – people who can help you, you want to reach out to and connect with

- ✓ Get yourself a brilliant coach

- ✓ Get yourself a brilliant mentor

- ✓ Have an accountability partner from now on

Check out www.newmanagersecrets.com/resources

Alison Miles-Jenkins

CONCLUSION: HOW TO GUARANTEE YOUR SUCCESS

So my job is almost done. I've shared 20 chapters of proven and practical skills, techniques, knowledge, tips, tricks and shortcuts to being a great manager. I've given you 20 sets of top takeaways which you can start implementing immediately as well as prompts, exercises and cheat sheets to enhance your actions. Notice I didn't say action planning. It's not about the planning; it's about the doing.

I want to congratulate you for setting aside a day (or perhaps a bit longer depending on your reading and learning styles and daily pressures) to read this book. It suggests that you truly want to have a successful management career and be a great manager for the people who are in your team. It also tells me that you didn't pick up this book because you are comfortable or satisfied with where you are in your career currently.

I'm guessing you want to change or improve your current position. So take action. Be determined. Be persistent, relentless even. You will get to where you want to go.

One thing I would say is don't just read this book once and go on with business as usual. Keep it handy and refer to it often. Remember, the things you've learned in this book are the same secrets and techniques I've shared with 1000s of other managers in face to face training and coaching sessions over the years.

Once this book is available to millions, I know it's going to be almost impossible to work with everyone who wants more one to one support to fast track their management career. So I've created something special just for you as a reader of this book. I've opened up space in my private Accelerate programme so that I can personally spend some time with you on the phone, online, and face to face to help you fast track where you want to go.

If you'd be interested in being part of Accelerate, then I want to invite you to apply to me personally. You can apply here by emailing me:

alison@leadinglightlearning.com

Once you've applied, you will get a call to discuss the programme and see if it's a good fit for us both. If it is then we could actually be talking less than a week from now!

Here's to your success.

Alison x

London 2016

PS Don't listen when someone says: you can't. You can.

ABOUT THE AUTHOR

Alison Miles-Jenkins BA (Hons) FCIPD is founder and Chief Executive of Leading Light Learning, which has evolved from Training To Achieve, the award-winning learning and development consultancy she set up in 1990. She has 30 years' experience in people development. She is seen as a powerful and unique resource and is respected, renowned and sought-after by those looking for the best in people management and development. Alison has helped more than 45,000 people achieve individual, team and organisational goals through her programmes, consultancy and coaching, in the UK and internationally. As a Corporate & Executive and Personal Performance Coach she has helped key contributors, managers and leaders across all sectors to overcome work challenges and make the most of opportunities, professionally and personally.

Her success has won her many accolades including Better Business Awards, Finalist of one of the Businesswoman of the Year competitions and Winner in November 2010 of an Education and Lifelong Learning Award. Alison is a regular contributor to professional magazines and journals, has been featured on the BBC and is in demand for speaking engagements throughout the country. She is author of the book "New Manager Secrets" published in 2016.

She is a graduate of Warwick University, has numerous post graduate management qualifications, is a Fellow of the Chartered Institute of Personnel and Development and has taught Chartered Management Institute courses at the highest level. Alison is married, with three grown up children, four dogs and a horse.

Printed in Great Britain
by Amazon